Achieving Success for Kids

Achieving Success for Kids

A Plan for Returning to Core Values, Beliefs, and Principles

Tim L. Adsit

ROWMAN & LITTLEFIELD EDUCATION

A division of

ROWMAN & LITTLEFIELD PUBLISHERS, INC.
Lanham • New York • Toronto • Plymouth, UK

Published by Rowman & Littlefield Education
A division of Rowman & Littlefield Publishers, Inc.
A wholly owned subsidiary of The Rowman & Littlefield Publishing Group, Inc.
4501 Forbes Boulevard, Suite 200, Lanham, Maryland 20706
http://www.rowmaneducation.com

Estover Road, Plymouth PL6 7PY, United Kingdom

Copyright © 2011 by Tim L. Adsit

All rights reserved. No part of this book may be reproduced in any form or by any electronic or mechanical means, including information storage and retrieval systems, without written permission from the publisher, except by a reviewer who may quote passages in a review.

British Library Cataloguing in Publication Information Available

Library of Congress Cataloging-in-Publication Data

Adsit, Tim L., 1948–
  Achieving success for kids : a plan for returning to core values, beliefs, and principles / Tim Adsit.
    p. cm.
  Summary: "*Achieving Success for Kids* is a clarion call to action and explains why we need to save America's children and return our nation and our schools to the core values, beliefs, and principles upon which our nation was founded. Tim L. Adsit presents a visionary blueprint for change and success in achieving and exceeding international standards in American schools"— Provided by publisher.
  ISBN 978-1-61048-590-6 (hardback)—ISBN 978-1-61048-591-3 (paper)—ISBN 978-1-61048-592-0 (electronic)
  1. Public schools—United States. 2. Educational change—United States. 3. Education—Aims and objectives—United States. 4. Values—Study and teaching—United States. I. Title.
  LA217.2.A28 2011
  371.010973—dc23
                                                    2011025884

"If we ever forget that we are a nation under God, then we will be a nation gone under."

—*President Ronald Reagan*

This book is dedicated to God, to the story of Gideon found in the Bible, to saving America's children, to returning our nation and our schools to the core values, beliefs, and principles upon which our nation was founded. The place where world change begins is America, and, as Mohandas Gandhi said, "We have to be the change we wish to see in the world."

"America must be a country that is committed to creative collaboration and networking if it is to survive, thrive, and ride the wave of the future. America must go beyond the realm of assumptive thinking and welcome and embrace the dawn of innovation (and change) because there is nothing more empowering than an idea whose time has come." (paraphrased from a Successories wall poster, Successories, Inc., 2000)

Contents

Foreword		xi
Preface		xv
Acknowledgments		xix
Executive Summary		xxi
Chapter 1	The Problem: How and Why We Must Strive to Reach International Education Standards	1
Chapter 2	Introduction to the Solution	9
Chapter 3	Solutions: Ten Key Points of Action	15
Chapter 4	Immediate Action Recommendations For Business	17
Chapter 5	School Structure Changes	19
Chapter 6	Curriculum Changes	23
Chapter 7	Lesson Design and Staff Evaluation	29
Chapter 8	Assessment and Managing Education for Results	41
Chapter 9	Parental Involvement	45
Chapter 10	Self-Esteem and Self-Image-Training for Success	47
Chapter 11	Teacher Training and Development	49
Chapter 12	Foreign Languages Required	53

Chapter 13	SCANS Report on Skills Required for the Twenty-first Century—What Work Requires of Schools—Foundations for Success in the Twenty-first Century	55
Chapter 14	Two-Year Action Plan To Reach National Education Standards	73
Chapter 15	Two-Year Action Plan To Reach International Standards	79
Chapter 16	The Founding Fathers' Beliefs on Leadership	83
Chapter 17	What Works in Education: A Research Synthesis	87
Chapter 18	Effective Schooling Practices	91
Chapter 19	What Makes Some Schools and Teachers More Effective?	93
Chapter 20	The Common Principles of Essential Schools	103
Chapter 21	Summary	107
References		109
About the Author		113

Foreword

Since Tim Adsit released advanced copies of *Achieving Success for America's Kids* in April 2011, the word has spread, and he has been deluged with requests for the book once it is published by Rowman and Littlefield Education.

Advanced copies have been requested by business leaders and labor representatives; family and community members; parents, grandparents, and guardians with kids still in school, ESD and Boces superintendents, local school board members and school administrators, school site councils, teachers from across the nation; local, county, and state government officials; and governors, state superintendents of public instruction, state and federal legislators, and candidates for the upcoming 2012 elections.

Editorials praising the book's frankness and refreshing, no-nonsense clarity, simplicity, good sense, usefulness, provocativeness, patriotic overtones, self-critical assessment of the state of America's educational system from a former public school teacher and administrator, and clarion call to action to achieve international standards in America's schools are sure to follow.

Teachers have told the author that the book should be studied by every present and future member of the teaching profession.

Unlike most education research and many reports, *Achieving Success for America's Kids* was addressed to the American people and appeals to them to take action. It provides accurate and actionable information about a strategic plan that works and that will help all public or private American schools reach or exceed international standards in two to four years, and it does so in a form that is accessible to all education system stakeholders.

The book contains and links the reader to some of the best research about what works when it comes to educating kids. The information in this book is a distillation of a large body of scholarly research in the field of education.

Principals, master teachers on special assignment, team leaders, professors, and department heads anticipate using *Achieving Success for America's Kids* for staff development and courses they teach.

It is anticipated that school boards across the nation spurred to action by the contents of the book will promulgate policies to fully implement its recommendations. It is also anticipated that national educational labs will develop workshops to train school personnel to use *Achieving Success for America's Kids* with administrators, teachers, and parents.

Clearly, the American people know a good thing when they see it, and the author is heartened by that. But even though the preliminary response has been overwhelmingly positive, Tim is sure that there will be critics. They may complain that *Achieving Success for America's Kids* tells only part of the story; that its real purpose is to divert attention from the federal education budget; that it just rehashes old research that everybody already knows; that it is written by an evangelical Christian, fiscal and political conservative, who is only interested in getting a particular candidate elected in the 2012 presidential election; and that it only helps white, middle-class kids.

Achieving Success for America's Kids does leave some things out. It is not an encyclopedia on the subject and the ways to meet or exceed national and international standards of education; it was never meant to be. *It simply tells most of the story, perhaps the most important part.* And this book updates information left out of the original 1992 *Saving America's Schools—Blueprint for Change* booklet and video that inspired this book, in part. As for the budget criticism, readers will differ on the appropriate level of federal funding. But the fact remains that if we want to give our American children a good education that meets or exceeds international standards, we have to do the things described in *Achieving Success for America's Kids*. We can spend all the money in the world, yet if we do not do the kinds of things outlined in this book, we won't get the education results our youngsters need and deserve.

Some critics may say that the book simply repeats things we've known for a long time. Common sense asks, then, why haven't all American schools implemented these plans? They have been around and known about since 1992. Why are many schools and their students still achieving below national and international standards?

Perhaps people need to be reminded of "what everyone knows"; common sense has to be reinforced at times and acted upon. The author's purpose in *Achieving Success for America's Kids* is to make this happen so that our nation's practices correspond to "what we do know how to do."

Others may mutter that this book leaves disadvantaged youngsters out of the plan. Quite the contrary. Many of the findings and suggestions in Adsit's book come from "effective schools" research that was conducted primarily to determine what kinds of schools help poor, disadvantaged, and minority children the most. The author knows these things can work for those children.

People from all political persuasions ought to find recommendations in the book they can agree ought to be implemented. The findings and recommendations in Adsit's book can help all children learn more and meet or exceed national and international educational standards so they will be more competitive and productive in the twenty-first-century global, information-age economy.

Achieving Success for America's Kids makes sense of American education and talks about it in terms that the American public can understand. Adsit wants to make the best information available to the American people, and this book is a significant part of that effort. It ought to be read by all Americans concerned about saving America's kids and meeting or exceeding international standards in all American public and private schools.

Doug Wead, April 28, 2011

Doug Wead is a presidential historian and former adviser to two American presidents, a New York Times *bestselling author, an educator, and an independent business owner.*

Preface

"Hail thou mighty man of valor, fear not, for the Lord is with you, go in your power and save your country."

—Judges 6 and 7, KJV

"Remain independent of any source of income that will deprive you of your personal liberties." "There's no time to rest when there's work to be done. Eat on the run, forget about sleep, and change horses often." "If you're ridin' ahead of the herd, take a look back every now and then to make sure it's still there." "Too much debt doubles the weight on your horse and puts another in control of the reins (like China, like OPEC, etc.)." "Never run from a fight, if you're gonna get hit, it's better to take it in the front than in the back—and it looks better." "Don't let so much reality into your life that there's no room left for dreamin'." "If you work for a man, ride for his brand. Treat his cattle as if they were your own." "You can never step in the same river twice." "Pick the right horse for the job."

—Texas Bix Bender, *Don't Squat With Yer Spurs On! A Cowboy's Guide To Life*

"Those who believe it cannot be done need to get out of the way of those who are doing it."

—Unknown

As I stated in the dedication, this book is dedicated to God and to the story of Gideon found in the Bible in Judges 6 and 7, where a messenger appears to Gideon and says, "Hail thou mighty man of valor, fear not, for God is with you, go in your power and save your country."

And that is what this book, this clarion call to action, is mainly about: explaining why we need to save America's children and return our nation and our schools to the core values, beliefs, and principles upon which our nation was founded.

The book briefly examines and refers the reader to the founding fathers' beliefs on leadership; looks at what works in education; provides a research synthesis; provides pathways to excellence and making schools more effective; demonstrates how to manage education for results; describes how to cut costs and generate revenues in education not solely dependent on taxes; describes why and how small schools, education, and the importance of community are demonstrating pathways to improvement and a sustainable future not only for small schools but for all schools; and presents a bold, visionary blueprint for change and success in achieving and exceeding international, world-class standards in American schools within the next two to four years, restoring America and its educational system to their rightful place of prominence and leadership in the world in all subject and skill areas as identified in the SCANS Report found in chapter 13.

America's current educational system fails our children, by and large. They cannot compete with many children from information-age and other industrialized nations in the twenty-first century.

It is time for all stakeholders in America's failing educational system to stand up and make the changes necessary to regain our rightful place in the world as number one in all areas. Business and labor; families and communities; parents, grandparents, and guardians; ESDs/Boces; local school boards; school site councils; local, county, and state government officials; governors, state superintendents of public instruction, state and federal legislators; and the U.S. Secretary of Education, the current president, and presidential candidates for the upcoming 2012 election need to come to consensus quickly, mutually agree upon a course of action, and heed this clarion call to action.

Why? The internal health of our country and our very productivity as a nation is based upon education, and by and large, our system is failing miserably with a few notable exceptions. The *Nation At Risk* study warned us about this many years ago. Our nation is still at risk today! The statistics are worse now than they were when the *Nation At Risk* study came out. We must do something about our country's growing crisis in education. It is time to meet and discuss the problems facing American schools and to fashion a solution to these problems, a blueprint, and a duplicable and practical template for solving those problems in the next two to four years.

A commonsense, practical, workable blueprint is needed to quickly move American schools to meet or exceed international academic standards. This frank, clear, straightforward, provocative treatise lists proven strategies and concrete steps that can lift our children not only into international academic parity but also to a position of leadership and prominence. The United States is capable not only of reaching international standards but also of exceeding those standards in all categories and subject areas measurable in public and private education. The time to act is long past! But it is still not too late if we act now! I challenge all American stakeholders to take action now and to get involved in changing our American schools for the better.

It will take all of us working together to rapidly create these vital changes in American education. It may take legislation from the federal level with the funding to make it happen.

However, top-down change must not be followed by more unfunded mandates from either the federal or state level.

We need to downsize our federal government and work for more local control at the regional, state, ESD/Boces, district, and local school levels. We need less government and lower taxes! I am confident it can happen!

People in America have launched powerful movements and made powerful changes during the last century to address injustice, inequities, and intolerance, expand our knowledge and information, improve our technology, and overcome other threats to our quality of life, safety, and security. Now, we must become involved in very rapidly, and radically, reforming our educational system. This reform must be systemic in nature, not piecemeal, band-aid-type reform. We do not need some splash-and-dash type intervention and training program, but continuous progress in student learning and achievement stimulated and spurred on by year-around staff development programs for all staff including certified, classified, confidential, and administrative. Every school must be and develop its learning community. We must raise our standards.

Our nation's children depend on us. It's time to save America's children and achieve or exceed international standards in American schools. "If it's going to be, it's up to me (we) . . . (take responsibility for changing your country's education system now)." "Today's decisions are tomorrow's realities. Starting is half done! Take care? People who take care never go anywhere. Take a chance! Take charge! Take control!" "Don't kill the dream, execute it" (paraphrased from Robert H. Schuller Sr., *Tough Times Never Last, But Tough People Do!*).

Keep separate church and state, but return America's schools to a nation under God as our founding fathers intended. Say prayers in our schools again. Place "In God We Trust" over entrances to our public school buildings. Salute the flag every day. Recite the Pledge of Allegiance together as a class or school while standing. Allow prayer rallies and gatherings around the outside flag poles in front of American schools. Invite pastors to graduation and baccalaureate services and encourage them to give prayers to start or close the ceremonies. Post the Ten Commandments on the classroom walls of

American schools. Observe all patriotic American holidays. Call Christmas break by its intended name and not some politically correct interpretation—winter break. Stop worrying about being "politically correct."

Tell secular humanists and the ACLU to go straight to hell where they most likely will end up if they don't change their ways, beliefs, and attitudes. Realize that America's public schools are in a fight for the hearts, minds, and souls of our children every day. Join me in returning our public schools to the core values, beliefs, and principles our founding fathers intended our public schools to be based on. Honor America's veterans and invite them to assemblies to speak and tell our students why freedom isn't free and that people are dying for you and for me on freedom's frontlines daily, both at home and all over the world.

Incidentally, if any of these suggestions seem a little radical or if any of these suggestions are currently against the law, then fight to change the laws and elect people to public office that support these beliefs and who will vote to change these laws at the local, state, and federal levels. That is the American way! American patriots must stand up and be counted now, just like the tea party in Boston many years ago. Be strong, be fearless, and just do it, knowing that "Those who wait on the Lord, shall renew their strength; They shall mount up with wings like eagles, They shall run and not be weary, They shall walk and not faint" (Isaiah 40:31, KJV).

Acknowledgments

I would like to acknowledge Associated Oregon Industries for giving written permission to reprint portions of the report titled *Saving America's Children: Achieving International Standards in American Schools—A Blueprint for Change*. The original idea for this book is based, in part, on their 1992 report.

I would also like to acknowledge Doris Spencer, one of my former administrative assistants, who did some of the word-processing for me.

Finally, I would like to acknowledge Dr. Willard Daggett, who is a noted New York teacher, lecturer, and one of the original contributors to the 1992 report *Saving America's Children*. Dr. Daggett provided me with some of the more up-to-date academic statistics comparing U.S. achievement to other countries of the world.

Executive Summary

The United States is mistakenly attempting to recreate the "Schools of Our Youth"; many of us baby boomers attended school during the *Leave It to Beaver* years. Times have changed. We cannot continue to strive for our grandparents' curriculum, which focused on an industrial-age model of schooling, but instead, we must quickly institute strategies for the needs of remaining a leader in the global economy and the information-age model of schooling and skills needed for the twenty-first century of which we are a part.

Approximately 19 years ago, *Partners For Success: Business and Education* jointly dispelled the myth that poor and minority students couldn't learn. *Partners For Success: Business and Education* is a now somewhat outdated report and video describing the work of a respected group of school principals who guided underachieving schools to nationally recognized academic success, including two where I had the privilege to serve, Harrisburg Union High School District U-5J, located in Harrisburg, Oregon, and Perrydale School District No, 21, Perrydale (Amity), Oregon.

The school principals' 10 essential elements for achieving success and their 2-year plan for turning around a failing school were distributed nationwide for others to emulate. See the 2-year plans as presented in chapters 14 and 15 herein. Most of the statistics presented in this original report are old but still relevant, only the performance of most American schools has gotten worse since 1992, not better.

The return on the investment in American schools and school children versus the gains in achievement and productivity needs to improve greatly. "America does not have a lack of money problem or other resources; rather, it has a lack of creative ideas problem" (Adsit, 2005) and has visibly, consciously, and deliberately moved into a state of secular humanism, moral decay, and decline, and moved away from the core values, beliefs, and principles upon which this nation and its schools were founded. (Read the books by Donald T. Phillips, entitled *The Founding Fathers on Leadership: Classic Teamwork in Changing Times* and *Lincoln on Leadership: Executive Strategies for Tough Times*.)

Our schools must return to teaching lifelong guidelines for growing responsible citizens such as trustworthiness, truthfulness, personal best, active listening, and no put-downs; likewise, life skills such as caring, common sense, cooperation, courage, curiosity, effort, flexibility, friendship, initiative, integrity, organization, patience, perseverance, pride, problem solving, resourcefulness, responsibility, and sense of humor must be taught, modeled, nurtured, and developed. (Materials for teaching these lifelong guidelines and life skills have been developed by Susan Kovalik and Associates, www.kovalik.com; skovalik@oz.net, 33506 10th Place S., Federal Way, WA 98003. Distributed by Books for Educators, 1-888-777-9827.) I have personally led schools and districts that have implemented these materials, and I know from experience that they work in improving school climate and in growing responsible student citizens in the areas mentioned above.

Another program that works for developing character and improving achievement is a program entitled "Character and Competence," by Lynn Scoresby. "Character and Competence" can expand a teacher's range and skills at bringing out those qualities parents and teachers hope for most. It can enable a teacher to capture unused motivation and direct an entire class toward the development of character, achievement, and improved learning. It begins with a unique view of competency and includes a teaching model that integrates processes natural to human growth with the educational experience of the classroom. This combination joins teacher and students in a remarkable relationship that adds power to the process of achieving and promotes the qualities we seek in the lives our students. For more information about these publications, contact Knowledge Gain Publications, Ph: (800) 526-7793; Fax: (801) 225-9498.

Incidentally, the reader should note that I have no personal, monetary interest in either one of these programs, but I know that they work, and that is why they are mentioned here.

Now, in 2011, these same partners that were brought together in the 1992 *Saving America's Children* study and report are challenged and encouraged to come back together under the leadership and funding of concerned, independent business owners, bringing business and educational leaders from all stakeholder groups together, including public and private school administrators, school board members, school and district site councils, district budget committee members, legislators, governor representatives, certified teacher employee groups, classified staff groups, parents, PTA representatives, and student representatives from at least grades 5 through 12; city, county, and state Department of Education representatives and Boces/Education service district representatives need to come together with themselves and with 5 to 10 carefully selected international experts to outline what changes are needed in America's schools.

If we ever hope to have our children achieve international parity and eventually exceed and lead existing world standards in all areas of education in the twenty-first century, now is the time to respond to this clarion call to action! Wake up, Americans! By failing to plan and act now, we are planning to fail and have more failure in achieving or exceeding international education standards in American schools in the future!

"It doesn't take a hero to order men into battle. It takes a hero to be one of those men who goes into battle" (General H. Norman Schwarzkopf, from a television interview with Barbara Walters, March 15, 1991).

Further, when one talks the talk, good leadership demands that one also be willing to walk the walk. I am volunteering to help strategically plan, develop, implement, lead, evaluate, and report the results of such a symposium, but I will need some principal underwriting from interested and selected business partners who read this book and wish to help save America's kids.

These stakeholders and carefully selected outstanding educators must be willing and able to unite and collaborate to develop specific practical, useful, and mutually agreed-upon methods and standards our American schools can apply immediately to obtain more effective levels of achievement in all academic areas for our school children.

Why would these experts from competing countries wish to assist America? Success breeds more success. Competition is healthy and good, and creative collaboration is even better, especially for those competing for use and control of finite resources, products, and services the world over. Sharing leadership, knowledge, and technology can help solve many of the world's current challenges. Working together, everyone achieves more!

Key points must be developed at this newly proposed symposium or education summit, similar to those outlined in the original report developed some 19 years ago, such as the following:

- Business and school partnerships are needed to achieve an internationally competitive school system;
- Structural changes are necessary to ensure the delivery of an internationally competitive school curriculum for the twenty-first century;
- Effective assessment tools are needed to ensure all students have the opportunity to develop their potential to meet and exceed international education standards;
- Parents must be involved to ensure their children receive the best possible education;

- American students' self-esteem and self-image must be developed in an internationally competitive school system using mutually agreed-upon programs and processes to accomplish that working closely with the home, faith-based organizations, and the school;
- Teacher training and development is a critical factor in achieving an internationally competitive school system. Learning communities must be established in every school in the nation and all employees, not just teachers, should receive training and staff development;
- Foreign languages must play a vital role in an internationally competitive school system and be made part of graduation requirements.

(Original source: *Saving America's Children: Achieving International Standards in American Schools—A Blueprint for Change*, Associated Oregon Industries, Salem, Oregon, and National Association for Schools of Excellence, Portland, Oregon, 1992, pp. viii–x)

All American children can reach this goal of meeting or exceeding international, world-class standards, but not on the same day, in the same exact way. Students must be allowed to proceed at their own level and rate of learning. This will require a carefully developed philosophy of education such as the one posited below:

Education must be personalized. Alternative learning options must be developed and implemented which match a teacher's teaching styles, personality types, and social styles to student learning styles, personality types, and social styles.

Personalized education is a systematic effort on the part of the school to take into account individual student characteristics and effective instructional practices in organizing the learning environment.

All learning is entirely personal. Readiness and incentive, rate of learning, preferred methodology and content—all vary widely from person to person. Every learner has unique abilities, experiential backgrounds, and learning, personality, and social styles. No two learners are necessarily ready to learn at the same time, on the same day, in the same way, or to the same degree. Learning for each individual is, to an extent, unique.

Philosophically, a personalized view of education requires that we accept students where they are (intellectually, socially, emotionally, and physically) and help them to progress at their own rates and at an optimal level for their capabilities.

Instructional planning should be based on an analysis of student characteristics. In my opinion. It should use the effective lesson design developed by Dr. Madeline Hunter from UCLA. To do so would move education away from the traditional assembly-line, batch-processing model to a personalized one. Programs could then be based on the appropriate differences that exist among groups of learners rather than on the assumption that everybody learns the same way.

Personalized education is a match of the learning environment with the learners' knowledge, processing strategies, concepts, learning sets, motivational systems, and acquired skills, and it is a continual, cyclic process.

Under this philosophy of education, the teaching cycle becomes one of Diagnosis-Prescription-Instruction-Evaluation (DPIE). In diagnosing the learner, the focus is on developmental characteristics similar to those described by Havighurst and Erickson, learning styles as described by Gardiner, and learning history. In prescribing, the focus is on advisement, goal setting, planning, and program placement. In instructing, the focus is on study and thinking skills as outlined in Marzano's work, and on materials, methods, time, and teaching style. The teacher's teaching style must be matched to the student's learning style for optimum learning and achievement to occur.

School days must be lengthened. The greater the time on task, the greater the achievement gain. (See research by D. Berliner, September 1983; J. Brophy, 1979; W. Hawley and S. Rosenholtz, with H. Goodstein and T. Hasselbring, Summer 1984; J. Stallings, 1980; and H. J. Walberg, 1984.)

And, in evaluating, the focus is on program effectiveness, teacher performance, and student progress. This model of education incorporates the best of research-based strategies and proven classroom instructional components while leaving the mode of implementation to the individual, locally controlled school or district. It is both structured and flexible. It suggests a total teaching/learning plan for all students, but requires no one approach for all.

Through this unique meeting or symposium being suggested herein, a systematic review of American education will be completed. The information gleaned from these international experts and stakeholders will result in specifically proven strategies and models that, when fully implemented, can and will move any American school into the international arena of excellence, productivity, and high achievement.

In addition to the identification of specific strategies, a process and action plans for implementation must be developed to provide practicing educators with a twenty-first-century blueprint for change.

With this blueprint, American schools and communities serious about implementing real change now will have the resources to meet the demands of twenty-first-century society and its workplace.

Leadership from the federal, regional, state, and local levels must work hand in hand to pass legislation that jump starts and implements these recommendations.

Furthermore, limited federal funding should be distributed utilizing existing funding models presented in Oregon and other leading states educationally based on a weighted funding formal and model.

Philosophically, we must have more accountability and mutual agreement, less federal and state control and unfunded mandates, standards and policies. Targets need to be established to reduce all federal, regional, state, ESD/Boces, and district paperwork and reporting, and eliminating all those positions now associated with this reporting frenzy, by at least 80 percent.

Federal, regional, state, ESD/Boces, and local districts must not mandate something through law, policy, or administrative rule if they are not, in turn, willing to fund it. Instead, we must have more local control at the regional, state, ESD, local district, and school site council levels, and give these entities a stable and predictable baseline of fiscal support they can depend on and strategically plan on from year to year despite what is happening with shortfalls in revenue, or the economy, and so on.

As I stated above, it is time to act! We must not only talk the talk, but we must be willing to walk the walk! The stakeholders in American education need to collaborate, cooperate, and mutually agree upon a clear course of action for change and improvement in American education. We need to do something, and I challenge you to lead, follow, or get out of the way of those of us trying to cause the changes that most, if not all of us, know must inevitably occur.

Current research clearly shows the knowledge, skills, and attitudes being taught to American students have little relationship to those necessary for success in today's society and working world. That is amazing and deplorable!

Why are American school children falling behind the rest of the world? I believe the answer lies in several areas that are correctable, if acted upon immediately, and that is why I wrote this book and what is described in the remainder of it.

Consider the following, as both quoted and paraphrased from the original participants who wrote the *Saving America's Children: Achieving International Standards in American Schools—A Blueprint for Change* report mentioned previously:

1. American children spend significantly less time in school than their peers internationally.
2. American society does not have a clear understanding of the purpose of its elementary and secondary education. (We need a clear, concise, and mutually agreed-upon vision and mission statement, set of core beliefs and values, goals, objectives, and performance indicators for our elementary and secondary schools.)
3. The United States ranks tenth in the world compared to other industrial nations in pupil expenditure, kindergarten through grade 12, as compared to per capita GNP. In 2011, the United States spends an average of $10,000 per pupil and in New York, for example, they spend $14,000 average cost per pupil.

4. American parents universally agree that our current system of education is in desperate need of change and repair in America, yet only a small percentage believe their child's school is in need of assistance.
5. The curriculum in American schools consists of courses designed to be independent of each other, while research suggests that adult life is primarily an interdependent exercise.
6. Our children rank highest in the industrialized world in television viewing and lowest in time spent reading. In 2011, American students currently rank fourteenth in the world in reading achievement; seventeenth in science achievement, and twenty-fifth in math achievement. (As reported on *Huckabee*, Fox News.com, 5–6 p.m., PDT, April 17, 2011.)

    There is simply no excuse for American students to rank that low in relation to other major industrialized, information-age countries. As a nation and as an educational establishment, we ought to be ashamed of our current levels of achievement and national performance. An excuse is simply a skin of a lie stuffed with reason. I, for one, am tired of hearing excuses, and I want to see results and action, not any more excuses!
7. Children see little relationship between what they do in school; and what the rewards from school could be. (Paraphrased and quoted directly with written permission from *Saving America's Children: Achieving International Standards in American Schools—A Blueprint for Change*, presented by Associated Oregon Industries and National Association for Schools of Excellence, 1992.)

Even though much of our existing curriculum may be appropriate, the skills stressed when mastering its content do not mirror the skills necessary for effective competition in the upcoming decade and beyond. As stated earlier, recreating the schools of our youth will not adequately prepare our children for the new basic skills and technical and professional knowledge required by all in a modern, information-age, global economy and society. To be competitive, America's schools must change. American schools must raise their standards to those considered to be international, world-class standards.

We must measure our progress with both formal, commonly accepted and comparable assessments and informal assessments. We must be more accountable to those that are paying the bill. Since 1970, we have tripled the amount we spend on education at the federal level. Currently, $77 billion is being spent on education in 2011, and yet, we have not received triple the gain in achievement and productivity. Instead, we continued to decline in achievement. The return on the U.S. taxpayers investment is not good, to say the least, currently in American schools.

"If it ain't broke, don't fix it" used to be the cry and conventional wisdom back in the industrialized model of schooling. Now the rallying cry in the twenty-first century must be "If it ain't broke ... break it!" As John A. Young, then president and CEO of Hewlett-Packard Company, said, "It's more than entertaining reading; it's survival skills in these times of breakneck change" (Robert J. Kriegel and Louis Patler, *If It Ain't Broke, Break It*).

America's schools are trapped, like gerbils on a wheel, in a system that fails to recognize and reflect global changes in technology and the speed of impact of these changes in the employment world. American education is battling to protect the heritage of our traditional school structure instead of developing cyclic, systemic, and continuous progress strategies and techniques to compete in the international community. We must act now to create a school system that will develop an educated citizenry able to compete internationally as the world continues moving into the first part of the twenty-first century.

Ours must be a uniquely American solution to an American challenge (problems are only challenges and opportunities in disguise). We must not fall into the trap of adopting the Japanese, the British, the Swedish, the German, the Canadian, or the Chinese approach exclusively. Rather, we must take the best of the best and integrate it into America's approach and strategic plan.

We must identify the best of the best from across the world where their children are meeting or exceeding world class, international standards, and integrate their models and ideas into our American educational system. The original group of outstanding educators who participated in the International Education Symposium in 1992 outlined an answer and plan that has worked for those that have implemented it, this author being one.

In the final analysis, no excuse for failure is acceptable for our American schools and students. Success is the only option! We are in a competitive, information age, and so far, our schools, by and large, are failing. To use an analogy, America needs to repair the jet airplane (our educational system) while it is in motion, creating and manufacturing new parts or entire planes where necessary, robbing and cannibalizing spare parts from models of jet planes that are working, and refueling, all while still in motion.

We must change! Now, let's examine in some detail, what needs to be done and why.

Chapter 1

The Problem

How and Why We Must Strive to Reach International Education Standards

> "There is no such thing as a problem, only challenges and opportunities in disguise. There is a seed of equal or greater benefit in every adversity. When faced with a mountain, I will not quit! I will keep on striving until I climb over, find a pass through, tunnel underneath, or simply stay and turn the mountain into a gold mine, with God's help!"
>
> —Reverend Robert H. Schuller Sr.

The world of the twenty-first century is waiting for our American students to complete school, but before American children can join their counterparts and competitors in the modern-day, information-age workplace and perform their jobs, our educational system must make sure it has done its job. Will our American children be ready?

In this chapter, I intend to take a clear, frank, critical look at what, in my opinion, is the deplorable condition of most of America's public schools, to take a brief look at how well our schools our serving our youth, and to offer a practical and workable "Blueprint for Change," a template that can be successfully duplicated quickly in any public or private school in America.

As mentioned previously, information and data mined from International Education Symposium participants back in 1992 resulted in proven strategies that can move any American school into the international arena of global competition and excellence.

But these symposium participants did more than simply develop strategic plans. They also outlined a detailed implementation process with timelines to provide educational practitioners with a clear, concise, and workable road map to excellence and meeting or exceeding international education standards. As a result of this earlier work and the updated information I have provided in this book, schools and communities serious about implementing real change now have a significant resource to take American education from where it is to where it needs to go, confidently and boldly, in the twenty-first century.

As a parent, community leader, educator, or independent business owner reading this book, you ought to be concerned, as I am, about how well today's school children will fit into today's and tomorrow's work force. As I am aware, our children's cultural development and exposure to the arts is essential to their balanced experience of life. However, if our children do not have the high skills demanded by the business world today, their lives will have little fulfillment or enrichment; instead, they will have low wages.

Our American children face technological realities our educational system has not prepared them for. The question is, is our American educational system keeping pace with technology? Unfortunately, in my opinion, the answer is no.

The fact is that America, along with the rest of the civilized world, has rapidly shifted from an industrial-based society and economy to one based on technology and information. The impact of this change is being felt throughout our nation's current work force and our economy, and a lot of this technology is apparently being ripped off from America by our competitors, especially China, Russia, South Korea, and Japan. Can you blame them? Not really. They just want to be competitive also; however, the playing field must be level with free trade, a balance of imports and exports, and no games to try and devalue each other's currency. This fact is being reported upon, almost weekly, in national newscasts and in the leading newspapers. In many competitors' eyes, America and its leaders are viewed as a joke rather than as a respected nation and leader of the free world as we once were, and as we are capable of being again in the near future. For example, take a closer look at our country's major employment sectors:

- Agriculture accounted for 85 percent of the American work force in 1900, but only 3 percent in 1989.
- Production/manufacturing accounted for 73 percent of the domestic work force in 1959, but only 18 percent in 1989. By the year 2000, as little as 2 percent of the work force was employed in this sector.
- The Service sector employed 44 percent of our work force in 1989, and this sector is rapidly becoming automated. As the number of jobs decrease, the skill levels necessary to fill available positions will go up.
- The Information sector is growing. In 1992, it employed 35 percent of the American workforce. By the year 2000, it employed roughly 44 percent.

Based on these figures, it's easy to see which skills would be appropriate for our American school children to be learning. The question is, are they?

Think about this: By current educational standards, high school–equivalent graduates in Europe and Asia are approximately 10 years behind current technology. By comparison, the U.S. is roughly 20 years behind. Is this disparity being felt?

In 1980, America had the highest paid workers in the world. In 1990, we were 12th. And by the year 2000, the U.S. ranked no higher than 25th" (noted by Dr. Willard Daggett, noted New York teacher, lecturer, and educational consultant, in *Saving America's Children: Achieving International Standards in American Schools—A Blueprint for Change*, p. 2).

Certainly, numerous factors contribute to this situation. But broadly speaking, the reason America has fallen so far behind the pace of technology, by and large, is because we haven't yet begun to teach the basic concepts, principles, and technical systems that are the foundation of the coming generations of technology.

One reason our public school curricula are insufficient in America is because of an insistence on teaching courses rather than applicable skills. This is an important distinction, particularly in view of the requirements for competency and success in the workplace of the twenty-first century. (See, for example, the skills outlined in the federally funded SCANS report found in chapter 13 of this book.)

In the year 2000, 44 percent of all workers in the United States were involved, in some way, in the information industry. In other words, nearly half the nation's work force is collecting, analyzing, synthesizing, storing, and retrieving data.

Now, what skills do you imagine would be the most beneficial for young people in America to have when they're ready to enter the work force? Skills derived from outmoded classroom instruction? Or application skills, including an ability to work with information systems, a solid background of technical reading and writing, and an ability to frame questions in words for doing daily research on the Internet that will help in doing your job?

The answer is obvious and rhetorical. But this doesn't mean America's educational model is necessarily wrong, just incomplete. We are falling further and further behind the rest of the industrialized world.

In fact, you might find it alarming to learn just how far behind we've fallen. I know it alarmed me and I found out about it and started doing something about it in earnest way back in 1992 while serving as the superintendent/principal in Perrydale School District 21, Perrydale (Amity), Oregon. That school became a quality small school of excellence, as it continues to be today. It has received local, regional, state, and national recognition.

For example, in 1969, measuring the literacy levels of 18 to 24 year olds, the U.S. was ranked first in the world. By 1979, the U.S. had sunk to twenty-first. By 1989, we ranked 49th (*Saving America's Children*).

Ironically, America's overall domestic literacy rates haven't dropped, the rest of the world has simply passed us by because they are preparing their young people for the workplace in the twenty-first century, and we're not.

In 1989 and 1990, American industries hired more than one million foreign-born and foreign-educated young people, with the equivalent of a high school education, to fill top-paying entry level positions. These young people understand information systems and technical applications; most of America's young students don't.

If our U.S. businesses could have found Americans with the necessary skills to do the job, would they have hired them? Certainly, but American high school graduates, by and large, do not possess the desired academic or technical skills.

Even worse, an increasing number of U.S. students are simply dropping out of school. The dropout rate in America's secondary schools is four times higher than any other industrialized nation. This is totally inexcusable, deplorable, and unacceptable. The 4-year college dropout rate in the U.S. is 58 percent, as compared to 11 percent in most other industrialized nations. And the dropout rate in America's 2-year colleges is almost 70 percent!

For those who don't drop out, the modern workplace presents a number of severe challenges. For example in 1989, 46 percent of our high school graduates were qualified for only 2 percent of available entry level positions. That statistic has not changed much today (*Saving America's Children: Achieving International Standards in American Schools—A Blueprint for Change*, presented by Associated Oregon Industries and The National Association for Schools of Excellence, Copyright 1992, p. 3).

More up-to-date statistics since the time of the original report in 1992 show:

- "The U.S. ranks 21st out of 30 comparable nations in science literacy;
- 25th out of 30 in math literacy; and
- 15th out of 29 in reading literacy" (D. Koretz, "How Do American Students Measure Up? Making Sense of International Comparisons").

One reason for this is there seems to be little, if any, relationship between what is taught in our American classrooms and what our young people need to know and be able to do to compete successfully in the working world. As a result, unless the United States makes some serious "systemic," system-wide changes in our current educational system, the rest of the world will be filling a larger and larger percentage of America's work force.

Who's going to be left out? Our American children. Who will fill the low-paying jobs? Our American children. Come on, American leaders and stakeholders in America's educational system. I challenge you to rise up, put your money and creative ideas where your mouth is, and act by working together as a team to cause the changes necessary to meet or exceed international standards of education in the next two to four years. Don't point fingers and be negative. Don't take the easy way out and be tempted to blame the teachers and their unions or the administrators or the parents. It's easy to criticize, condemn, and complain and offer no solutions; most fools do. Rather, let's collaborate to solve the challenges facing American education.

Continuing technological advances mean that the modern work force is growing smaller and at the same time becoming more highly trained. Because of the rapid evolution of automated systems, robotics, and information networking, the world's production/manufacturing, service, and information industries need workers with increasingly specialized skills, but they need fewer of them.

The main point is simply this: Our educational system lags severely behind the rest of the world in teaching the skills necessary to function successfully in today's technological, information-driven workplace. American has been told this and we have known this for at least the past 19 years, and very few schools, districts and states have done much about it. What's more, there is tremendous competition for even the lowest-paying jobs our high school graduates are qualified for.

If America's young people are to compete and survive in today's workplace, the American communities and businesses that depend on a highly educated and skilled work force must assume a more active role in assisting our educational system to identify and teach vital skills.

Parents must also take a more active role in helping to redefine America's educational system. They must continually challenge and help their children meet or exceed new academic standards. Our American students will rise to the level of expectation set for them. This is true for our staff in American schools as well. I found the above statements to be true in the schools I had the privilege to successfully serve in as a teacher and lead as a school administrator for over 38 years.

It is vital that we renew our appreciation and respect for the incredibly difficult job our country's teachers and classified support staff have undertaken, often in overcrowded, underfinanced schools.

We must support America's teachers and administrators, who are committed to children and to the rapid changes we must make in our American educational system. Those that don't support this change need to be deselected from the organization and certainly not given merit pay. If we continue to do what we have always done in American education, we will continue to get what we have always gotten and are continuing to get in many schools. We simply must change!

It's clear what needs to be done here in my humble opinion: either get on the bandwagon or get off and go into some less important kind of work. Educating America's kids is certainly one of the most important endeavors, if not *the* most important, you can and ever will be involved with, at least in a secular sense. Why not give it your absolute best, your all?

It's been my observation that in addressing the need for change in our public schools, it's not that we are not working hard or willing to work hard; it's just that the way we are doing it doesn't work. There is a difference between working hard and working smart. We're doing one heck of a job, America, on the wrong thing! Let's get back on track, work as a team, and do the right things to save America's kids and to put a blueprint for change in place, which is clearly outlined in this book, that will allow all American schools to achieve or exceed national standards in the next two years and international, world-class standards in two more years after that.

What will eventually cause those working within America's schools to accomplish the needed change? When we choose to do this, we will find that there's no limit to what can be accomplished if it doesn't matter who gets the credit. A very wise man named Les Giblin once said,

> We are all egotists. We are all more interested in ourselves than in anything else in the world. Every person you meet wants to feel important, and to amount to something. There is a hunger in every human being for approval. A hungry ego is a mean ego. Satisfy the other person's hunger for self-esteem and he/she automatically becomes more friendly and likeable. Unless you do love, yourself in the sense of having some feeling of self esteem and self-regard, it is impossible for you to feel friendly toward other people. Remember, low self-esteem means trouble and friction. Help the other fellow like himself better and you make him easier to get along with. People act or fail to act largely to enhance their own egos. (Les Giblin, *How to Have Confidence and Power in Dealing With People*)

We must give our school board members, local school site committees, school administrators, teachers, support staff, students, parents, business leaders, community patrons, the faith community, and all the other stakeholders involved as partners in America's educational system a reason to act to largely enhance their own egos. What greater reason to act could we possibly have than the one I am suggesting herein? We must all work together toward the common goal of saving America's kids. Arguing against that reason is like arguing against mother, apple pie, and the flag!

In the interim, until this plan for saving America's kids is fully implemented, our educational system must begin now to place greater emphasis on critical thinking, problem-solving, decision-making, the dynamics of human relations, building our students' self-image and self-esteem, and other important independent skills as outlined in the SCANS Report included in chapter 13 of this book.

If we continue measuring academic achievement, by standardized testing, let us, at least, insist that subjects addressed in testing include: (1) independent applications found in the SCANS report, *What Work Requires of Schools*; and (2) technical reading and writing and the ability to manipulate information systems.

Otherwise, we'll simply be measuring the ability to pass tests, and not the ability to successfully pass through the doors of the modern workplace both at home and abroad. To keep our children in American competitive, we must be ready and willing and able to implement dramatic changes in our schools now! Are you ready to do that? If not, why not?

Chapter 2

Introduction to the Solution

"The significant problems we face today cannot be solved at the same level of thinking we were at when we created them."

—Albert Einstein

Dr. Willard Daggett, noted New York teacher, lecturer, and educational consultant, wrote this section in the original *Saving America's Children* report, and it has been reprinted here in its entirety with written permission from those who hold the copyright:

"If you're going to get serious about educational system change in . . . your individual communities across the nation, you've got to have a systematic plan . . . and the first step is awareness.

"You've got to create public awareness programs with your faculties and with and with your communities. If you don't do that, you will not change the conditions that need to be changed, nor have the ability to impact the American student's ability to compete in the international arena.

"After you have an awareness program, you've got to get really serious about the question: What is the role of school?

"I believe most teachers don't believe what they teach has anything to do with being prepared for employment. I would go further and suggest many teachers don't believe they have anything to do with preparing lifelong learners. Oh, I'm sure most schools believe our kids should be good citizens, and that's the role of the schools. Anybody want to tell me what a good citizen is? Is it voting in the last election? Does that mean over half of Americans are not good citizens?

"See, we use terms like 'good citizenship,' and we never even define what we mean. And if we haven't defined the specific skills needed for the various adult roles we're preparing our children for, how are we ever going to be held accountable? So, we need to carefully define the skills out children are going to need to successfully compete, and live, in the adult world.

"The next step is to define the negotiable and non-negotiables. We need fundamental school reform, and I don't personally believe that fundamental school reform can be legislated, or at least that legislation alone is sufficient by itself to create workable school reform.

"You first must have a willingness to change, a belief, a desire. So, what is negotiable, and what isn't? Is the school year non-negotiable? No. Okay, who's willing to pay the extra 30 percent to get us somewhere close to where other nations are? Taxpayers? Or are teachers willing to work 30 percent longer with no additional pay? Is a 30 percent increase in taxes non-negotiable? If it is, make the public say it. Are our disciplines, the sanctity of our disciplines, non-negotiable? Or can we get rid of selective courses?

"My position is, we've got to decide what's negotiable and what isn't before we can get serious about school reform. Because if we don't create an agreement as to what we are willing to negotiate, we can't change effectively. And every affected group, from parents to teachers, administrators, the general public, business people and politicians and, of course, our children, must be participants in this process.

"Once you know the ground rules, you must develop a plan, otherwise you will be in danger of simply recreating the schools of your parents' and grandparents' youth.

"If the preceding steps are handled properly, the final step is relatively easy. You rewrite curriculum. You rewrite assessment. You retrain teachers. It's not going to be easy, but it is doable. We've got the resources. We've got to learn how to manage change, and we need a plan that will work; a plan that will move us from where we are to where we want to go.

"Again, to do that, we need awareness, we need to identify the purpose of our schools, and we need to define what skills our graduates are going to need to not only survive, but prosper in the adult world.

"The fact is, if we don't change, the human and economic consequences are going to be astronomical" (*Saving America's Children: Achieving International Standards in American Schools—A Blueprint for Change*, Dr. Willard Daggett, "Introduction to the Solution," pp. 6–7).

To Dr. Daggett's remarks above, I would simply add the following:

- What is our vision for American public schools in the twenty-first century? I believe the vision for American public schools is to develop competent future citizens of character capable of lifelong learning in the twenty-first century.
- What is the mission for American schools in the twenty-first century? I believe that the mission of American schools in the twenty-first century is

to continuously improve student learning and achievement of those skills, knowledge, and attitudes required for success in meeting or exceeding international, world-class standards.
- In America, we must move from a reactive orientation (problems/crisis) to a proactive orientation (vision); we must move from a focus on practice (inputs and processes) to a focus on student performance (outcomes); from individual action to collegial action; from short-term improvement efforts (goal setting) to long-term, systematic efforts (goal attainment); from perception-based decisions to data-based decisions; from use of craft knowledge alone, to use of research and craft knowledge; and from individual/district responsibility to school district/school and individual responsibility.
- "The very essence of all power to influence lies in getting the other person to participate." (Harry A. Overstreet)
- In a change of the magnitude being suggested in this book, one not only has to make people aware, as mentioned by Dr. Daggett above, but one also needs to survey and measure the Conditions of Readiness to Change with those who are responsible to carry out the change. J.T. Pascarelli from Northwest Regional Educational Laboratory is credited with developing such a survey instrument in February 1985. These conditions include the following:

Cluster I—Accessibility of Resources and Support
1.1 Extent and kind of technical knowledge needed to implement the change
1.2 Availability of technical knowledge within the school
1.3 Accessibility of technical knowledge and expertise outside the school
1.4 Availability of financial resources
1.5 Support from key administrators in the district

Cluster II—Internal Press for Change
2.1 Proportion of individuals who are dissatisfied with the present situation
2.2 Proportion of individuals who value the proposed target, vision, mission, goals, and objectives
2.3 Proportion of individuals who have confidence that the proposed change will bring benefits

Cluster III—Stability of Staff Undergoing Change
3.1 Proportion of turnover of staff membership
3.2 Commitment of key administrators to remaining in current positions for the duration of the early stages of the change
3.3 Proportion of individuals attempting other changes

3.4 Proportion of the staff experiencing stress due to the complexity of the school organization

Cluster IV—Skill in Collaborative Group Work
4.1 Group skill in communicating accurately
4.2 Group skill in making clear decisions
4.3 Group skill in conducting effective meetings
4.4 Group skill in working effectively with diverse views, opinions, and values
4.5 Group skill in solving problems

Cluster V—Norms Supporting Collaborative Group Work
5.1 Norms supporting collaboration
5.2 Norms supporting continued communication in emotional situations
5.3 Norms supporting individual disclosure of feelings, worries, or frustrations with the task
5.4 Norms supporting third-party helping

Cluster VI—Spirit of Risk-Taking
6.1 Proportion of individuals who are willing to risk new action on behalf of the school
6.2 Willingness of key administrators to make reciprocal changes in their behavior, modeling the change they wish to see
6.3 Presence of charismatic leadership
6.4 Proportion of individuals willing to undergo training in new skills and behaviors
6.5 Proportion of individuals experiencing stress, anxiety, or threat, regardless of the source

Directions: Each of these conditions of readiness to change should be placed in a survey and a place to mark relevant or not relevant should be placed to the right side of each condition. A place should also be made for discussing and summarizing the results of your analysis. And a place should also be provided for writing down the implications for action in your specific building or district.

- Likewise, Dr. Shirley Hord and others from the Southwest Educational Development Laboratory wrote an intriguing book entitled *Taking Charge of Change* (1998). The following is paraphrased and excerpted from that book:
  - With respect to the initiation of change, there must be a "felt need" by local users and the users must select the solution.
  - During the implementation stage of change, increase capacity for change; involve local users; allow for school/program mutual adapta-

tion; allow for ownership and internalization of the change; allow for practice time and training using the desired change; fit management practices to the innovation and situation; teachers must be involved in the use of the innovation and in carrying it out; principals must be committed and must support teachers and the innovation or change being implemented; plan for quick, visible results during the initial stages of implementation to boost staff morale and show success; success breeds success and recognition and reward need to accompany successfully making the changes desired; and provide for teacher practice time in implementing and utilizing the newly implemented change.
- Key assumptions of the Concerns Based Adoption Model include: Change is a process, not an event; change is accomplished by individuals first, then institutions; change is a highly personal experience; and change entails developmental growth in both feelings about skills in using new programs.
- Purkey and Smith examined school improvement variables that must be present for lasting change to occur: school site management; instructional leadership; staff stability; school wide staff development; district support; collaborative and collegial relationships and (mutual respect); and a sense of community.
- Elements which increase satisfaction and increase the desire to invest further effort in the change process include achievement; recognition; interesting work; responsibility; advancement; and growth possibility. (Remember what Les Giblin, cited earlier in this book, said: "People act or fail to act largely to enhance their own egos." The above elements, which increase satisfaction and increase the desire to invest further effort in the desired change process, would seem to verify Mr. Giblin's statement.)
- Elements which reduce satisfaction but not the desire to invest further effort include policy/administration; technical supervision; salary/working conditions; status; job security; effects on personal life; and interpersonal relationships.
- Psychological motivating factors that affect change include feelings of competence; feeling a sense of belonging; feeling a sense of usefulness; and feeling a sense of potency as a result of the change.

Chapter 3

Solutions

Ten Key Points of Action

"Two people with belief and convictions are equal to a force of 99 with an interest."

—Pastor Jim Buckley, Shoshone Idaho

"Never doubt that a small group of thoughtful, committed citizens can change the world. Indeed, it is the only thing that ever has."

—Margaret Meade

"Try not, there is no try. There is only do or do not. Do it!"

—Yoda, as quoted by
Doug Wead, presidential historian

"Do It Now (DIN)."

—Dexter Yeager

"Make it happen! You can do it if you put your mind to it!"

—Author Unknown

"Beginning is half done!"

—Reverend Robert H. Schuller Sr.

During the course of the original International Education Symposium held in 1992, mentioned earlier in this book, participants were asked to respond to eight key questions, each of which addressed a specific component of an overall plan for helping America's schools reach international educational standards. The following was developed as a direct result of information distilled during and after that symposium. It is excerpted, paraphrased, and quoted here by written permission. In addition, I have added two additional key points of action based on my experience with implementing the original plan.

The 10 Key Points of Action:

1. Business and school partnerships are needed to achieve an internationally competitive school system;
2. Structural changes are necessary to ensure delivery of an internationally competitive school curriculum;
3. Curriculum changes are necessary to ensure international requirements are met;
4. Effective assessment tools are needed to ensure all students have the opportunity to develop their potential to meet and exceed international education standards;
5. Parents must be involved to ensure their children receive the best education;
6. Student self-esteem must be developed in an internationally competitive school system;
7. Teacher training and development is a critical factor in achieving an internationally competitive school system;
8. Foreign languages play a vital role in an internationally competitive school system (*Saving America's Schools*, 1992);
9. Lesson design and staff evaluation; and
10. Teacher training and development.

These 10 Key Points of Action will be discussed in greater detail in the chapters that follow.

Chapter 4

Immediate Action Recommendations For Business

Immediate actions recommended for business include the following:

1. Business and school partnerships are needed to achieve an internationally competitive school system. In order for our students to be competitive in the future, businesses must develop partnerships with schools. Accountability and planning are vital because these are the expectations that business people have. First, business involvement in schools must be contingent upon schools having a strategic plan for children quickly reaching national and international academic standards. Following that, businesses should take these actions:
   - Business and industry must take an active role in defining what competency levels are necessary for specific technical and professional occupations.
   - Business and schools must join in partnerships to provide work experience for students and internships for teachers.
   - Business people must sit on school advisory and board positions.
   - Businesses must provide resources for teaching basic entry-level work force skills.
   - Businesses must provide awards to effective schools.
   - Business and schools must enter into technological information sharing services.
   - Businesses and schools must create transferable high school academic credit for on-the-job work experience.
   - Businesses and schools need to establish programs showing students a direct relationship between school performance and work performance.

Chapter 5

School Structure Changes

Structural changes are necessary to ensure delivery of an internationally competitive school curriculum.

- Schools must be structured in a way that permits teachers to teach appropriate curricula. "Right now, schools are organized based upon the Taylor concept of management; scientific management. Basically this is a top-down model, everything broken into individual parts. Courses are mutually exclusive, independent of each other. Somehow, we've got to move toward what American business is moving toward, which is the Deming Model (systems model) of management, where everything is interdependent and nothing is dependent. Our schools and especially our testing programs drive everything to be independent and mutually exclusive of each other. We've got to change this, because the skills our learners are going to need later on are all interdependent. They're all interdisciplinary" (Dr. Willard Daggett, *Saving America's Children*, p. 10).
- The length of the school year must be increased to match other industrial countries. "Of all the industrialized nations in the world, the United States has the shortest school year. We go 180 days (on average). Again, comparing our school year with the Japanese, their school year lasts 243 days. While we go 180 days, our average number of absentee days is 20, meaning that we're really in school only 160 days. In Japan, and this is based on diaries that were kept, the average number of absentee days per year was three. Therefore, we're actually comparing school years of 160 and 240 days. I'm not recommending that we emulate the Japanese system. I'm only pointing out the huge disparity between our two systems and asking you to consider the probable differences in the preparedness of our

system's graduates compared to those from Japan" (Dr. Willard Daggett, *Saving America's Children*, p. 10).
- The length of the school day needs to be expanded. "In grades kindergarten through six, the average American child is in school 25.2 hours per week. At the other extreme, a school child in Japan attends for 38 hours per week. In our middle school grades, seven through nine, the American school week is 28 hours long. In Japan, 46 hours. And at the high school level, American kids are in class 26 hours per week. Japanese high school kids, 41.5 hours" (Dr. Willard Daggett, *Saving America's Children*, pp. 10–11).
- Offer alternative pathways to high school graduation encompassing professional and technical education, with built-in flexibility between pathways that enables individuals to move easily between academic, technical, and professional education. (This plan has been successfully implemented in Oregon for many years now.)
- Structure professional and technical training to prepare students for the needs of high-tech industry, as well as adult life. We are changing from a lifelong employment system based on school qualifications to a professional vocational society based on skills and skill-related attainment levels (*Saving America's Children*, p. 12).
- Implement primary school programs that allow children to progress at their own developmental pace, such as the non-graded kindergarten through third grade concept.
- Schools should provide assistance to students and families. Head Start has demonstrated the effectiveness of this comprehensive approach. It addresses the employment, housing, health, and vocational needs of the families of preschool children. In fact, it is recommended that preschool programs such as Head Start be made available to all children, so every child will come to school prepared to learn.
- Life experiences should be negotiated for high school (and I might add college) academic credit, if you've acquired skills and knowledge, maybe through a hobby or spare-time activity. If that has relevance to a particular vocational activity, you can be accredited for that. We have to be able to assess and accredit prior learning and experience (*Saving America's Children*, p. 14).
- Individuals with unique training outside of conventional education should be given the opportunity to teach.
- Educators must be able to make curricular decisions on a site-by-site basis and be held accountable for those changes (in reaching or exceeding international standards).
- Class size should be flexible, depending on the expectations of the learning activity.

To these original recommendations from the 1992 symposium, I would add that the following school structural changes are necessary to ensure delivery of an internationally competitive school curriculum in the twenty-first century:

- We need to build on the strengths, people, and programs that already exist, unless that structure and combination of people are not working. If the structure and combination of people are not working then we need to change the school's structure and mix of people.
- As Dr. Shirley Hord and others say in their book entitled *Taking Charge of Change*, "Change is a process, not an event, method, or a particular one-best approach. There is a process that must unfold in order for change, continuous learning and achievement, and school improvement efforts to be successful. Change must be understood in terms of what happens to individuals. Understanding how individual staff members and students respond to an innovation, for example, is critical to facilitating their continuous learning, to monitoring, and to institutionalizing that change or innovation.
- "Change is accomplished by individuals first, then schools and districts. Change for individuals is a highly personal experience. The personal perceptions, feelings, and frustrations of individuals are part of the change process. I have found that to initiate lasting change, there must be a 'felt need' by local users for the change, and the staff and students must be an integral part of selecting the solution if they are expected to implement the change whether the change is related, for example, to the essence of the teaching and learning process, to integrating technology in school programs or administrative functions, to implementation of the NCLB legislation, or Oregon's Educational Act for the Twenty-first Century, or other state's acts, and so forth.
- "The keys, once again, to all school improvement and change efforts are (1) involving local users (students, parents, teachers, administrators, other staff members, board members, and the community) in shared decision-making activities; (2) implementing processes to increase ownership and internalization like task force teams and focus group sessions on specific aspects of the innovation, change, or school improvement program; (3) allowing staff training and practice time to use the particular change or newly learned skill; (4) providing for quick, visible results; and (5) providing for long-term school-wide and district-wide staff development and training with respect to the particular change or innovation, as opposed to 'one-shot,' 'slash and dash' type in-service programs" (as adapted from S. Hord, W. Rutherford, L. Huling-Austin, and G. Hall, *Taking Charge of Change*).

- In our respective school districts across America, we must look at "what was" and "what is" before developing and building a mutually agreed upon plan and program for "what could be" and "ought to be" in the future. A leader, usually the superintendent, curriculum director, principal, teacher on special assignment (TOSA), or department head, subject-area, or grade-level specialist would lead the efforts to continue to build upon the positive foundation that has already been established. This leader would proceed at a pace that people are comfortable with; explore, evaluate, and implement any new or different ideas only after building upon the existing strengths of the current programs and human resources; and only after identifying and openly discussing identified needs for change, school improvement, and professional growth.

American Schools Need A Common Mission and Vision:
"Vision without action is merely a dream. Action without vision just passes the time. Vision with action can change the world."

—Joel Arthur Barker

The key is to focus on continuously improving student learning and achievement and meeting or exceeding international standards in all subject areas which is our major mission in American public and private schools in my opinion, and our vision is to develop competent future citizens of character for the twenty-first century.

Chapter 6

Curriculum Changes

Curriculum changes are necessary to ensure international requirements are met.

- An integrated curriculum must be developed including these basic skills: keyboarding, data manipulation, problem-solving, and decision-making, systems of technology, resource management, economics of work, human relations, applied math and science, and career planning.
- Reading, writing, listening, and speaking will be the primary focus in all content areas.
- Math areas stressed should be basic operations, logic, statistics, probability, and measurement. Algebra and geometry taught in isolation appear to be seldom used in the work force and everyday life.
- Applied science should be taught within an integrated curriculum. "Students from every course in the school must take basic skills in each of the other courses, so that students in mechanical engineering will take chemical and electronic engineering basics as well" (*Saving America's Children*, p. 20).
- Higher order thinking skills such as problem solving, analysis, synthesis, and evaluation (see Bloom's Taxonomy) should be emphasized at all levels and in all areas of instruction.
- Student work experience and apprenticeships with business and civic authorities should be required. Student participation in entrepreneurship courses and school-based economic development and student run businesses should also be required. See Tim Adsit's book entitled *Small Schools, Education, and the Importance of Community* (2011).
- The majority of instruction should focus on application and problem-solving skills.

- The majority of instruction should engage students in actively using information, rather than passively receiving information. (See the *Learning Pyramid* adapted from the National Training Laboratories, presented elsewhere in this book.)
- Children need to be taught and assessed by working together to solve problems and create solutions, much like adults do in the workplace. (Cooperative learning and problem solving is an important part of the workplace in the twenty-first century.)
- "What do we call it in American classrooms when kids work together on exams? Cheating! We need to make a major shift and begin integrating cooperative learning, teamwork . . . and to place a high value on the interdependency of the learning process" (Dr. Willard Daggett, *Saving America's Children*, p. 23).
- The availability of computers and emerging technologies must increase in classrooms, particularly at the middle school and high school levels.
- Curriculum for primary children must be developmentally appropriate and reflect that young children learn best through active involvement and play.
- At all grade levels basic skills should include the ability to use information systems, demonstrate personal and civic responsibility, model acceptable personal behaviors and skills, set priorities, demonstrate dexterity, work as a member of a team, reason, and use appropriate interpersonal skills.
- No textbook should be required as the sole source of meeting class requirements.
- Critical analysis and evaluation should be taught as prerequisites for entry level work, further education, and everyday life.
- All school must adopt distance-learning technologies. Using cable systems, internet capabilities, virtual schools (the Rosetta Stone program), and satellites, a teacher with specific skills can instruct students who are hundreds of miles away. Many rural schools currently do this, making classes in specialized areas such as physics, foreign languages, and other professional technical skills available to students everywhere.

As a superintendent, principal, and curriculum director for a good portion of my career, I have always been an instructional leader with knowledge of current research and best instructional practices including the integration of technology to meet all levels of academic and behavioral needs in the schools of the twenty-first century.

I have accomplished this through remaining informed about trends in educational research, thought and successful practice and sharing these ideas with others, through networking with colleagues and business leaders in civic groups and church groups, through actively supporting, contributing to, and attending professional organization activities, through attending and leading in services and staff development training opportunities, and by associating with people in the community both inside and outside the field of education.

For example, research on how students retain information tells us that our instructional methods must change. Why? Because average retention rates go up considerably when students teach others and make immediate use of learning.

Further, with the lecture method, students only retain 5 percent; through reading they retain 10 percent; through audio-visual methods they retain 20 percent; through demonstration they retain 30 percent; through group discussion they retain 50 percent; through practicing by doing they retain 75 percent; and through teaching others and immediately using what they have learned, they retain 90 percent. Good teachers already know about this research and are already changing their teaching methods and teaching style to methods that increase student retention and higher order thinking skills (*Learning Pyramid*, adapted from National Training Laboratories).

Curriculum must address the needs of all students and must be designed to permit them to see a clear relationship between what they do in school and what they will do in their adult lives. Much of our schools' current content is appropriate, but the skills stressed in mastering this content do not always mirror the skills necessary in adult life and work, at least in most schools.

This challenge needs to be overcome by identifying and implementing the skills for the twenty-first century as outlined in the SCANS report included in chapter 13 and working closely with business partners in achieving international standards of performance in those skill, knowledge, and attitude areas.

In addition to the recommendations mentioned by the original 1992 symposium participants above, in my opinion, the curriculum essentials of a modern-day educational system include the following: the ability to use language, to think, and to communicate effectively; to use mathematical knowledge and methods to solve problems; to reason logically; to use abstractions and symbols with power and ease; to apply and to understand scientific knowledge and methods; to make use of professional technical information and technology and to understand its limitations; to express oneself through the arts and to understand the artistic expressions of others; to understand other languages and cultures; to understand spatial relationships; to apply knowledge about health, nutrition, and physical activity; to acquire the capacity to meet unexpected challenges; to make informed value judgments; to recognize and to use one's full learning potential; to prepare to go on learning for a lifetime; and to participate in student activities, clubs, and so on to gain an understanding of team building, competition, character development, and getting along with others to reach goals that have been set.

I believe in maintaining a good balance between academics, professional-technical programs, the performing arts, remedial activities, enhancement activities, and student activities. We must keep America's children engaged before school, during lunch time, and after school through such activities. The busier and more engaged our American children are, the less time they will have to get in trouble by buying or selling drugs, experimenting sexually, and so forth.

By personal experience, I have found that the skills and competencies needed by successful change agents as they implement the plans for change outlined in this book include the following:

- *Personal skills in building relationships.* I am able to bring people together. I am a team player and a team builder. I am a reasonable and practical person. My style of leadership stresses my ability to lead, develop, and motivate, to delegate effectively, to build effective teams, to build consensus, and to resolve conflicts that may from time to time arise in any complex, dynamic organization. I possess the ability to encourage and engage others to do their very best work. As a change agent, you will need these skills also to be successful.
- *Modeling a strong work ethic.* I possess high expectations for myself and others, and I can inspire and motivate others to achieve mutually agreed-upon goals to not only maintain current progress and improvement of the past five years but also set new goals and action plans for the next five years. Motivation is an area in which I excel as a leader. For example, as a motivator, I am an individual who is able to inspire others to do their very best work by serving as a role model of excellence myself.
- *Possessing the skills to motivate and support employees and to help staff members make personal commitments to fulfilling the mission of the district.* My experience has demonstrated that several keys to being an effective motivator include these skills and abilities: (1) good communication skills; (2) serving as a good role model yourself and being willing to walk the walk instead of just talking the talk; (3) maintaining a positive mental attitude; (4) knowing how to delegate effectively and empower staff (this skill brings out the best in others); (5) skills in supervision and evaluation; (6) skills in staff development and understanding human psychology, social styles, and personality styles; (7) skills in team building, team management, shared decision-making, and conflict resolution; (8) the ability to set goals and maintain high expectations and a commitment to excellence; (9) and the ability to increase rigor and relevancy of coursework and be an enthusiastic, energetic, yet realistic, visionary able to motivate, encouraging

innovation and creativity in others to implement a shared vision of rigor and relevancy of coursework that continuously improves student learning and achievement.
- Being a leader with the strength to provide a sense of direction for the school district and a visionary leader who can demonstrate the ability to do successful and thoughtful short- and long-range strategic planning.
- *Communicating well with individuals and groups of people and enlisting their support in allowing this shared vision to become a reality.* I am a leader who has extremely high standards and expectations and a leader who will establish the same standards and expectations for all members of the school district. I am clear in defining priorities and goals, and I am a leader who is willing to be held accountable for achieving those goals while also holding associates, superiors, and subordinates alike accountable to a similar level of expectation. I can articulate the central values and goals of the school district and the community, and I am a person who can inspire others and create a culture allowing the various elements of the school district and community to work together toward attainment of those values and goals.
- *Possessing experience managing financial resources, facilities and construction; familiarity with bond measures and construction bonds.* I have had 38 years of successful experience in managing financial resources, facilities and construction, bonding, and construction projects. For example, I have had personal responsibility for budgets as large as $15.5 million–plus to as small as $450,000. I have served school districts as large as 12,500 students to as small as 60 students. I possess strong, proven skills in fiscal management and budget preparation. I know how to maintain the district's commitment to fiscal responsibility. I have many years of demonstrated, successful experience in relating the financial needs of the district to the community, state, and federal government's ability to raise funds and in implementing practical ideas to cut costs and generate alternative revenues not dependent on property taxes. In fact, I am known as a national expert in the area of school finance. I have also had many years of experience in conducting successful campaigns to pass bond and school plant facilities levies.
- *Possessing experience and success in seeking grants and alternative funding sources.* I have been a successful grant writer over my career, bringing in over $2,000,000 plus in grant funds. My book, *Practical Ideas for Cutting Costs and Ways to Generate Alternative Revenue Sources*, was published in May 2005; its sequel, the second edition, was published in 2011 and entitled *Cutting Costs and Generating Revenues in Education*. These books offer hundreds of practical ways to cut spending in education and to generate revenues not dependent solely on property tax dollars.

As I stated earlier, we don't have a lack-of-money problem in education in the United States; we have a lack-of-creative-ideas problem, in my opinion. Schools must become community centers, the local community and the world must become our curriculum, and we must stress school-based economic development and entrepreneurism. These ideas are developed in detail in my book entitled *Small Schools, Education, and the Importance of Community: Pathways for Improvement and a Sustainable Future.*

With the enrollment ups and downs of the last several years, one must be a good strategic planner and not only anticipate the trends apparent in enrollment data, but also be flexible in planning from year to year based on a well-established set of criteria, goals, core values, short-term and long-term strategic plans, and student-staffing mix formula. We must learn to anticipate, predict, and deal with change. I am an expert in this area, and you should be also.

We must be ready to honor our heritage while embracing change and the demands of the future.

As Dr. Robert Schuller Sr. says, "We must take charge and take control of our problems in order to look beyond our obstacles to creative solutions. Don't surrender leadership to outside forces. Today's decisions are tomorrow's realities" (*Tough Times Never Last, But Tough People Do!*).

Curriculum changes are necessary to ensure international requirements are met in American schools. And I believe that by returning to the core values, beliefs, and principles in American education that our founding fathers intended, the process of change will be facilitated. I know it has been for me during my career to date.

Chapter 7

Lesson Design and Staff Evaluation

Lesson design and the delivery of instruction in most American schools needs to be more effective, systematic, and efficient. The following model of effective lesson design and certified evaluation developed by Dr. Madeline Hunter and her associates at UCLA is recommended by this author.

Madeline Hunter's ITIP model for direct instruction may be found at www.hope.edu/academic/education/wessman/ . . . /hunter2.htm. The material below was adapted from this website.

Madeline Hunter developed a teacher decision-making model for planning instruction. Her model is called ITIP (Instructional Theory into Practice) and is widely used in school districts around the country. There are three categories which are considered basic to ITIP lesson design.

1. *Content:* Within the context of grade level, content standards, student abilities/needs, and rationale for teaching, the teacher decides what content to teach.
2. *Learner Behaviors:* Teachers must decide what students will do (a) to learn and (b) to demonstrate that they have learned.
3. *Teacher Behaviors:* Teachers must decide which "research-based" teaching principles and strategies will most effectively promote learning for their students.

When using Direct Instruction (DI) as the framework for planning, the teacher increases his/her effectiveness by considering the following seven elements as they "bring alive" the content or as they "scaffold" the learning needs of the students. Teacher decision-making is the basis of this approach to teaching. "Decide, then design" is the foundation on which all successful instruction is built.

The following excerpts are taken from "Planning for Effective Instruction: Lesson Design" in *Enhancing Teaching*, by Madeline Hunter, pp. 87–95.

When designing lessons, the teacher needs to consider the seven elements in a certain order since each element is derived from and has a relationship to previous elements. Also, a decision must be made about inclusion or exclusion of each element in the final design—not all seven elements will be included in every lesson. It may take several lessons before students are ready for guided or independent practice. When this design framework is implemented in teaching, the sequence of the elements a teacher includes is determined by his/her professional judgment.

1. (Learning Objective) Select an objective at an appropriate level of difficulty and complexity, as determined through a task analysis, diagnostic testing, and/or congruence with Bloom's cognitive taxonomy.
2. (Anticipatory Set) Motivate instruction by focusing the learning task, its importance, or the prior knowledge/experience of the learners.
3. State the lesson objective(s) to the students.
4. (Input) Identify and teach main concepts and skills, emphasizing clear explanations, frequent use of examples and/or diagrams, and invite active student participation.
5. Check for understanding by observing and interpreting student reactions (active interest, boredom) and by frequent formative evaluations with immediate feedback. Adjust instruction as needed and reteach if necessary.
6. Provide guided practice following instruction by having students answer questions, discuss with one another, demonstrate skills, or solve problems. Give immediate feedback and reteach if necessary.
7. Assign independent practice to solidify skills and knowledge when students have demonstrated understanding.

The following questions are from Madeline Hunter and can guide you in making teaching decisions.

1. What Instructional Input Is Needed?

All lesson design begins with articulation of an instructional objective. It specifies the perceivable student behavior that validates achievement of the precise content or process or skill that is to be the learning outcome. To plan the instructional input needed to achieve the target objective, the teacher must determine what information (new or already possessed) the student needs in order to accomplish the intended outcome. Students should not be expected to achieve an objective without having the opportunity to learn what is essential in order for them to succeed. Task analysis is the process by which the teacher identifies the component learnings or skills essential to the accomplishment of an objective. Once the necessary information, process, or skill has been identified, the teacher needs to select the means for "getting it in students' heads." Will it be done by discovery, inquiry, teacher presentation, book, film, record, filmstrip, field trip, diagram, picture, real objects, or demonstration? Will it be done individually, collaboratively, or in a larger group? The possibilities are legion, and there is no one way that is always best.

Examples:

** The teacher explains.
** A film is used to give information or demonstrate an activity.
** Students use library resources.
** Students discover the information by doing laboratory experiments or field observations.

2. *What Type of Modeling Will Be Most Effective?*

It helps students to not only to know about something but to also see or hear examples of an acceptable finished product (a story, poem, model, diagram, graph) or to observe a person's actions or hear him talk aloud about how he decided to perform a task (how to identify the main idea, or determine ways of thinking or making decisions while completing the assignment).

It is important that the visual input of *modeling* be accompanied by the verbal input of *labeling* the critical elements of what is happening (or has happened) so that students are focused on essentials rather than being distracted by transitory or nonrelevant factors in the process or product.

Examples:

** "I am going to use my thumb to work the clay in here like this so the tail has a firm foundation where it is joined to the body of the animal. In that way, it's less likely to break off in the kiln" (art instruction).
** "While I do this problem, I'll tell you what I'm thinking as I work" (math talk-aloud strategy).
** "Notice that this story has a provocative introductory paragraph that catches your interest by the first question the author asks" (literature instruction).

In lessons designed to produce divergent thinking or creativity, a teacher usually should not model because students will tend to imitate. The modeling should have occurred in previous lessons so that the students have acquired a repertoire of alternatives from which they synthesize an outcome satisfying to them—thereby being creative in their responses to the assignment.

3. How Will I Check for Understanding?

The teacher needs to know at what point students possess the information and/or skill necessary to achieve the instructional objective. The following are some ways of determining when and how.

SAMPLING

Sampling means posing questions to the total group, allowing them time to think, and then calling on class members representative of the ability strata of the group (most able, average, least able). This process focuses everyone on the generation of an answer and develops student readiness to hear an affirmation or challenge of his/her answer. Note that at the beginning of learning, correct answers are most enabling. Therefore, it is recommended that the teacher at first call on able students to avoid incorrect answers, which can "pollute" the learning that results from this approach.

Examples: State the question or give the direction, then give thinking time before naming a student to respond:

** "Be ready to summarize the results of _____."
** "What do you believe were the reasons that Washington was a great leader? I'll give you a minute to think."
** "How would you estimate the answer?"
** "What commonalities do you see?"

SIGNALED RESPONSES

Each member of the group makes a response, using a signal. For example, students show their selection of the first, second, third, or fourth alternative by showing that number of fingers, putting a pencil straight up for "don't call on me or this question," making a *c* with a hand when examples are correct or an *i* when incorrect. Math operations, first letters of words, and punctuation all can be hand-signaled. Nodding or shaking of heads, use of counting sticks, and pointing to a place in the book or to parts in a diagram or to objects are examples of the many signals that can validate learning, or lack of it, for each member of the group.

Examples:

** "Nod your head if you agree. Shake your head if you don't."
** "Signal whether you add, subtract, multiply, or divide, by making that sign with your fingers."
** "Show a *c* with your fingers if what I say is correct; an *i* if incorrect. Don't do anything if you're not sure."

** "Raise your hand when you are ready to answer this question."
** "On your microscope, point to _____."

GROUP CHORAL RESPONSE

After the teacher presents a question to the total group and gives thinking time, the strength of a choral response can indicate the general degree of student accuracy and comfort with the learning. However, this method usually does not give information about individuals.

INDIVIDUAL PRIVATE RESPONSE

A brief, written- or whispered-to-teacher response (when the teacher is moving about the room from desk to desk, table to table) makes students accountable for demonstrating possession of, or progress toward, achievement of the needed information or skills.

Examples:

** "Write the names of the three important categories we have discussed and one example within each."
** "Do the first part of this problem on your paper."
** "As I walk around, be ready to tell me your topic and the main idea of your paper."

4. How Will I Design Guided/Monitored Practice?

The beginning stages of learning are critical in the determination of future successful performance. Initial errors can become set and difficult to eradicate—called misconceptions. Consequently, students' initial attempts in new learning should be carefully monitored and, when necessary, guided so they are accurate and successful. Teachers need to practice with the total group or circulate among students to make sure instruction has "taken" before "turning students loose" to practice independently (with no help available). With teacher guidance, the student needs to perform all (or enough) of the task so that clarification or remediation can occur immediately should it be needed. In that way, the teacher is assured that students subsequently perform the task correctly without assistance rather than be practicing errors when working by themselves.

5. What Independent Practice Will Cement the Learning?

Once students can perform with a minimal amount of errors, difficulty, or confusion, they are ready to develop fluency, along with increased accuracy, by practicing without the supervision and guidance of the teacher. Only at that point can students be given an assignment to practice the new skill or process with little or no teacher direction.

Teachers, like doctors, are successful only when the student no longer needs them. All teaching has as its purpose to make the student as independent as possible. When lessons are carefully planned, student independence becomes much more probable. It is important that in independent work, the student does what already has been practiced rather than some *new*, or experimental, task. The purpose is for them to build confidence and competence in doing the task.

6. Should the Students Be Made Aware of the Lesson Objective and Its Value?

This element of an effective lesson involves communicating to students what they will learn during the instruction and why that accomplishment is important, useful, and relevant to their present and/or future life situations. It is *not* just the usual, "At the end of today's lesson you will be able to _____." Remember—not only the what, but the why!

Examples:

** "You were slowed down yesterday because you had trouble with _____. Today we are going to practice in order that you develop more speed and accuracy."
** "We are going to work on the correct form of letter writing so that you can write for the materials you need in your social studies project."
** "Today you are going to practice ways of participating in a discussion so each of you gets turns and you also learn from other people's ideas."
** "You are going to be surprised to find out what happened after Columbus returned and the difference his voyage made to our ways of thinking."

Note that the objective *as stated to the student* is not as it is stated in the teacher's plan book: "The learner will use correct form in writing a letter"; "The learner will list the results of Columbus voyage and explain their significance."

Usually, students will learn more efficiently if they know what the learning will be and why it is important in their lives. There are times, however, when the objective should *not* be known because it will distract them or turn them off. ("Today you are going to learn the difference between colons and semicolons" could elicit a "Who cares?")

7. What Anticipatory Set Will Focus Students on the Objective?

An "anticipatory set" results from a *brief* activity that occurs at the beginning of the lesson or when students are mentally "shifting" gears from one activity to the next. The purpose of an anticipatory set is to elicit students' attending behavior, focus them on the content of the instruction to follow, and help them develop a mental readiness (or "set") for it. The "set" may (but doesn't need to) include a review of previous learning if it will *help the student achieve today's objective*, but not routine review of old material. The set also may give the teacher some diagnostic data needed for teaching the current objective.

An anticipatory set activity should continue only long enough to get students "ready and set to go" so that the major portion of instructional time is available for the accomplishment of the current objective.

Examples: Examples of activities that produce an anticipatory set are having students—

** give synonyms for overused words when the current objective is improvement in descriptive writing
** create word problems to go with a numeral problem on the chalkboard when the current objective is meaningful computation practice
** review the main ideas of yesterday's lesson, which will be extended today
** state ways a skill might be useful in daily life when the objective is to develop fluency with that skill
** practice speedy answers to multiplication facts for a quick review before today's math lesson on two-place multiplication

An anticipatory set is *not* needed if students are already alert and ready to go because yesterday's teaching built a bridge or transition to today's lesson.

Summary—A Reminder

Not all the ITIP seven elements just described will be included in every lesson. It may take several lessons before students are ready for guided and/or independent practice. Also, the mere presence of an element in a lesson does not guarantee quality teaching. A teacher may use an anticipatory set that spreads rather than focuses students' attention ("Think of your favorite food; today we are going to talk about cereals"). Input may be done ineffectively. The modeling may be distracting ("I will cut this chocolate cupcake in fourths"). The seven elements are guides in *planning* for creative and effective lessons. They are not mandates!

Simply "knowing" the seven elements of planning for effective instruction will not ensure that those elements are implemented effectively. Also, simply having a knack with kids will not ensure the elements that promote successful learning will be included in instructional planning. Both the science and the art of teaching are essential. It is Madeline Hunter's belief, however, that deliberate consideration of these seven elements, which can promote effective instruction, constitutes the launching pad for planning effective and artistic teaching (using any model of teaching with *any* type of student) to achieve greater student achievement of *any* objective or goal.

Regardless of the teaching model, student success results from careful planning of how to bring the international standards alive, and through artistic implementation of the plan.

The intended purpose of the original work done by Dr. Madeline Hunter and her team at UCLA was standardizing an effective lesson design and providing improvement through staff development.

I believe that a modified version, which I have included below, entitled "Questions To Help You Analyze a Lesson," and which I have used successfully for years to evaluate teachers, is one model that has promise for adoption on a national level.

Why? "Questions to Help You Analyze a Lesson" focuses on research-based, effective lesson design and teaching. If this is what we want all teachers to know and be able to do, why not evaluate them, at least in part, on whether these elements are present in their teaching on the days they are observed? Of course, these elements may not be present in every lesson because there are different kinds of lessons, and in some states the processes, procedures, forms, and criteria for evaluation are mandatory subjects for bargaining and negotiations. My answer to this is, so what? Go ahead and bargain over them, come to a mutual agreement and understanding, and implement a process that is working and has worked successfully for years.

Certified Staff Evaluation Based on Instructional Theory Into Practice (ITIP)

Name _____ Employee Status: _____
                                                   Probationary—Permanent

Assignment: _____ School: _____

QUESTIONS TO HELP YOU ANALYZE A LESSON

Key: N/A = Not Applicable to Today's Lesson
   Yes = Observed Today
   No = Not Present, Not Observed Today

	N/A	Yes	No

A. STANDARDS
1. Did the students seem to know how they were expected to behave?
2. Did the class begin smoothly and efficiently?

B. INTEREST
1. Did the teacher relate this lesson to prior learning?
2. Did the teacher relate the learning to students' experiences?
3. Did the teacher provoke curiosity in the subject?
4. Did the teacher show his/her own interest in the lesson?

C. OBJECTIVES/PURPOSES
1. Did the teacher clearly state the objectives(s) of the lesson?
2. Did the teacher explain the reason for learning this skill or material?

D. PRESENTATION
1. Were the teacher's explanations clear and understandable?
2. Did the teacher provide accurate information?
3. Did the teacher explain any new vocabulary to students?
4. Did the teacher break down the new skill/knowledge into small steps?
5. Was the presentation appropriate to students' developmental level? (Concrete examples provided before abstraction)
6. Did the teacher use varied modalities (auditory, visual, tactile)?
7. Did the lesson move along briskly?
8. Were materials used purposefully? (e.g., pictures, films, transparencies, books, manipulatives)

9. Did the teacher model the desired new behavior? ___ ___ ___

E. INVOLVEMENT

1. Were all students required to respond to questions? ___ ___ ___
2. Did the teacher relate material to prior knowledge or experience? ___ ___ ___
3. Were students actively engaged in the lesson? ___ ___ ___

F. CHECK FOR UNDERSTANDING

1. Did teacher use questioning to determine if students understood? ___ ___ ___
2. Did teacher respond to nonverbal cues from students that they did not understand? ___ ___ ___
3. Did teacher encourage students to ask questions? ___ ___ ___

G. RETEACHING

1. Did the teacher use a different approach to reteach when students did not understand? ___ ___ ___
2. Did teacher provide activities for those students who understood while re-teaching? ___ ___ ___

H. GUIDED PRACTICE

1. Were directions for practice clear and precise? ___ ___ ___
2. Did practice relate directly to objectives? ___ ___ ___
3. Did teacher monitor performance carefully? ___ ___ ___
4. Did teacher provide immediate feedback as students practiced? ___ ___ ___
5. Did teacher adapt practice to meet individual students' needs? ___ ___ ___

I. INDEPENDENT PRACTICE

1. Did practice activities become homework? ___ ___ ___
2. Did homework relate directly to the objectives? ___ ___ ___

J. CLOSURE

1. Did the teacher review the stated objective(s) and purposes? ___ ___ ___

2. Did the teacher question students about their attainment of the objectives? ___ ___ ___
3. Did the teacher evaluate student learning? ___ ___ ___

K. MANAGEMENT

1. Was classroom environment orderly and organized? ___ ___ ___
2. Were materials ready prior to class beginnings? ___ ___ ___
3. Did teacher use time effectively? ___ ___ ___
4. Was teacher actively engaged with students most of class period? ___ ___ ___
5. Did teacher respond effectively to behavior problems? ___ ___ ___
6. Did teacher provide encouragement and support for positive behavior? ___ ___ ___

Supervisor's Recommendations and/or Summary Comments:

Teacher's Comments:

This is to certify that we have read and discussed the above report.

Identify attachments: _____

Pre-Conference: Date: _____ Time: _____ Place: _____

Observation: Date: _____ Time: _____ Place: _____

Post-Conference: Date: _____ Time: _____ Place: _____

_____

_____

Teacher's Signature   Date   Supervisor's Signature Date

cc: Employee
      Employee's File
      Supervisor's File

Chapter 8

Assessment and Managing Education for Results

> "School administrators and school teachers alike are responsible for their performance, and it is in their interest as well as in the interests of their pupils that they be held accountable. Success should be measured not by some fixed national norm, but rather by the results achieved in relation to the actual situation of the particular school and the particular set of pupils."
>
> —President Richard M. Nixon

> "What nobler profession than to touch the next generation, to see children hold your understanding in their eyes, your hope in their lives, your world in their hands. In their success you find your own and so to them you give your all."
>
> —Unknown

Students must be assessed on a regular, ongoing basis, but curricula should drive assessment, not the other way around. Assessment should include the following elements:

- A wide variety of assessment techniques such as anecdotal information (portfolios), assigned class work, oral questioning, quizzes, senior projects, tests, and standardized measures must be used.
- Letter grades and standardized achievement tests must not be used to assess student performance until after the first four years of schooling.
- Teachers and administrators must be assessed by how well their students learn and perform.

Education at all levels must be judged by how well it prepares students for the future. It is unfair to blame students and their families for the failures of American education.

As Daggett stated in the 1992 report and symposium mentioned earlier, "Try to forget your schools. Try to forget them for a while and think about our children. Because whether your sons and daughters wind up being accountants, attorneys, engineers, or technicians, whether they have no idea in the world what they want to be, they need a set of skills that simply are not now offered within the current American school structure. If we just focus on what kids need, we will change our schools. The gap is getting wide and wider between what our children need and what they're leaving school with; not because we're not working hard, but because society is changing faster than our schools" (Dr. Willard Daggett, *Saving America's Children*, p. 29).

ASSESSMENT AND MANAGING EDUCATION FOR RESULTS

> "Management is the acceptance of personal accountability determined by measurable results."
>
> "Every knowledge worker is, or potentially is, a manager. Counselor, educational technologists, librarians, and teachers as well as principals, and deans, superintendents and presidents must administer, plan, and lead if education is to produce effective results."
>
> —Richard W. Hostrop

> "Set Your Goals High, Then Exceed Them!"
>
> —David J. Schwartz

In addition to the original recommendations from the 1992 symposium mentioned earlier, from my own successful experience I recommend the following as some practical things districts can do immediately in improving student academic achievement for all students of diverse and special-needs backgrounds as well as regular students in all academic areas:

1. Raise academic expectations knowing that students and staff tend to rise to the level of expectation set.
2. Align curriculum to state, national, and world-class content and performance standards so we are teaching what is being tested.
3. Before students take state assessment tests, utilize practice tests and assessments patterned after the same type of tests that students would be

expected to take, and develop and implement alternative measures of performance not dependent solely on standardized achievement tests.
4. Improve students' test-taking skills and abilities.
5. Improve the district's test administration climate and overall conditions for testing.
6. Provide incentives for students to give their best performance on tests and recognize students who continuously improve above state/national standards.
7. Identify staff development needs in the particular content area and in the area of helping students to increase academic achievement, and target staff development and training to meet identified needs such as learning to use the various state scoring guides with students in the classroom.
8. Planning, developing, implementing, evaluating, and recording student work samples and performance tasks; using student portfolios, levels testing, and authentic student assessment techniques.
9. Aligning state content standards to day-to-day lesson planning and design using Dr. Madeline Hunter's Instructional Theory into Practice format presented elsewhere in this document.
10. Analyze desegregated test data at the sub-scale/strand level and identify areas in need of improvement. Identify teachers who consistently demonstrate strengths in these sub-scale score areas needing improvement and enlist their support in coaching and mentoring their peers regarding the instructional strategies they are using with students in their classrooms to continuously improve student academic achievement in these areas.
11. Use of technology in the form of computer-assisted instructional learning systems such as Accelerated Reader, which are proven to raise students' academic performance by as much as 1.5 to 3.0 grade levels per year in basic skills such as reading, math, social studies, and science.
12. Provide remediation and enrichment programs and services for those students who need it.
13. Provide awareness of the importance of improving student academic performance for all students by enlisting parent support for raising expectations, increasing academic learning time both in school and after school or at home, and stressing the importance of academic achievement at home.

There is nothing wrong with teaching to the test as long as the practice test reflects what we want students to know and be able to do in reaching or exceeding international standards.

Chapter 9

Parental Involvement

"Educating Everyone Takes Everyone."

—Slogan on a Badge-a-Minit in LaSalle, IL

"It takes a whole village to raise a child."

—African Proverb

Parents, grandparents, and guardians must all be involved to ensure their children receive the best possible education. Parents are the first and most important teachers their children have. Parents must play an active role in the education of their children, or they will greatly limit their future.

As the original *Saving America's Children* report stated in 1992:

- Parents must value school and school achievement, and they must encourage their children to do the same.
- Parents must monitor the progress of their children at all levels.
- Parents must drastically limit the amount of television their children watch, Research concludes children who watch more than 10 hours of television a week have lower school achievement, are less creative, and have smaller vocabularies (see *What Works: Research About Teaching and Learning*, 2nd edition).
- "The International Center on Comparative Studies shows that the average American child between the ages of five and 16 watches 19.6 hours of television a week. The next highest is Canada, at 10.2. And in Europe, the highest average in any of the European nations was seven hours a week. By comparison, American children spend an average of 1.4 hours a week

reading books. European kids . . . 7.8 hours per week" (Dr. Willard Daggett, *Saving America's Children*, p. 29).
- Parents must read to their children frequently from a very early age.
- Parents must frequently listen to their primary children reading.
- Schools should establish regular private consultation with parents to discuss progress, as well as techniques for incorporating supplementary home instruction.
- Some traditional parent involvement strategies must be continued: parent organizations, open houses, volunteer programs, and parent literacy classes for those who need it, taught in English.
- Parents should be members of school policy, oversight organizations, and local school site councils.
- Parenting classes must be provided for parents and be required for high school students.
- Schools should be willing to use the skills of the adults in their community, regardless of age (as adapted from *Saving America's Children*, pp. 29–31).

Chapter 10

Self-Esteem and Self-Image/Training for Success

"The greatest discovery of any generation is that a human being can alter his life by altering his attitude."

—William James

"Believe in yourself. You gain strength, courage, and confidence by every experience in which you stop to look for in the face. You must do that which you think you cannot do."

—Eleanor Roosevelt

"Hold an image of the life you want, and that image will become fact."

—Norman Vincent Peale

"When you sow an action, you reap a habit; when you sow a habit, you reap a character, and when you sow a character, you reap a destiny."

—Zig Ziglar

"Believe You Can Succeed and You Will." "Build Confidence and Destroy Fear." "Think and Dream Creatively." "You Are What You Think You Are." "Learn How to Think Positively."

—David J. Schwartz

"What lies behind us and what lies before us are tiny matters compared to what lies within us."

—Ralph Waldo Emerson

"Who you are today is the sum total of the choices you've made."

—James MacDonald

Student self-esteem and self-image must be developed in an internationally competitive school system.

- Self-esteem is built upon successfully achieving high individual standards.
- Schools must develop recognition programs that reward student achievement and effort.
- Teachers must help students build self-esteem by sincerely caring for them and guiding them toward genuine success on a daily basis.
- When students demonstrate success in international academic competition, celebrate their achievement both inside the school and with your external publics and the print and non-print media.
- "It is highly necessary for educators and teachers to have high expectations for all children, regardless of their family origins, race, sex, or socio-economic background" (Su Lin, China).

(As adapted from *Saving America's Children*, pp. 31–32.)

To these thoughts and recommendations from the original report cited earlier, I would simply add, *"Only you can change your life."* To accomplish much of anything, you need to integrate these five elements into your daily life:

- Belief in yourself
- A sense of purpose
- Action
- Discipline
- Perseverance (Bruce Garrabrandt, *The Power of Having Desire*)

Two outstanding resources come from Jack Canfield, co-author of the best-selling *100 Ways to Enhance Self-Concept in the Classroom*. Based on his successful work with over 100,000 teachers and 250 school districts, the curriculum guide and cassette-learning programs contain all of the newest methods and activities developed and tested since Jack's book was introduced in 1976. This is a 35-year-old program that is still effective today. *Self-Esteem in the Classroom: A Curriculum Guide* and *Self-Esteem in the Classroom: 3 Cassette/CD Album* help to build positive self-esteem in any age student, help to overcome negative learning blocks, create a positive learning environment anywhere, and motivate the unmotivated student (Self-Esteem Seminars, 17156 Palisades Circle, Pacific Palisades, CA 90272). *Chicken Soup for the Soul* is another very successful program. For more information, contact Teresa Esparza (800) 237-8336 ext. 41, or e-mail tesparza@chickensoup.com. You may also check out the following websites: www.souperspeakers.com or www.chickensoupforthesoul.com and www.jackcanfield.com.

Chapter 11

Teacher Training and Development

"If you can't teach with the Big Dogs, Stay Out of the Classroom."

—A picture and slogan on a coffee mug by Big Dog Sportswear, 2001

"Those that can, teach; those that can't should go into some less significant line of work."

—Unknown

"Give a man a fish and he will eat for a day. Teach him how to fish and he will eat for a lifetime. Tell me, I forget. Show me, I remember. Involve me, I understand."

—Chinese Proverb

"A teacher affects eternity; he can never tell where his influence stops."

—Henry Brook Adams

"A great teacher makes hard things easy."

—Ralph Waldo Emerson

"The world seldom notices who the teachers are, but civilization depends on what they do and what they say."

—Lindley Stiles

Teacher training and development is a critical factor in achieving an internationally competitive school system. These elements are essential for providing teacher trainees with the skills they need to become successful teachers:

- Teacher trainees must receive more on-site experiences in the working world.
- Teacher trainees should be taught by practicing master teachers. Teacher trainees must receive more training in classroom management.
- Teacher trainees should be trained using international standards and strategies.
- Teacher trainees must successfully intern for one year with an experienced master teacher before being certified.
- Outstanding retired master teachers should be able to work with school districts to act as trainers and mentors, without jeopardizing their retirement benefits or social security benefits.
- Each school and school district must provide a strong staff training program based on locally assessed needs.
- Successful teachers should conduct most teacher training.
- Training successful trainers should be recognized at each school.
- A rotating cadre of master teachers should be assigned for training statewide.
- Practicing teachers should be released and given paid sabbaticals for renewal training at least once every five years.
- Staff supervision should be conducted by master teachers.
- All teachers should be trained to teach writing, thinking, decision-making, and application of learning theory throughout the curriculum.
- Statewide in-service days must be provided. A minimum of 10 full-day in-service days is recommended (as adapted from *Saving America's Children*, pp. 32–35).

To these recommendations from the original symposium participants, I would add 8 Core Steps to Success as a Professional Learning Community Team Player interested in training, growing and developing personally, departmentally, school-wide, and district-wide that include the following:

- 100 percent use of your own personal brand of school products, goods, and services in entrepreneurial schools. Develop your personal, departmental, school, and district profit centers through in-home shopping services, as well as delivery, retail, wholesale, or independent business associate household gold programs and fundraisers.
- Develop your personal profit center through, class, grade-level, department, or program client and member sales, raising revenues not dependent

solely on property taxes to help offset the costs of school programs and teaching students entrepreneurship in the process.
- Activity—consistently and persistently share your program; market your brand, yourself, and your program. Be customer-service oriented in all classrooms, schools, and districts nationwide.
- Listen to a tape, CD, or DVD a day from school professional development system libraries and resource materials. Listen to, re-listen to, and give away tapes or CDs every day to others you are responsible for helping to grow and develop as team players. Keep cutting-edge and positive information flowing into your brain and your team. Positive in, positive out! Garbage in, garbage out!
- Attend all seminars, professional learning community meetings, and team meetings and events, whether at the departmental, school, or district level. Attend seminars and motivational events, and have others you are helping to grow and develop attend. Come, grow, serve, lead! Duplicate this pattern for success.
- Associate—become a team player. Working together, everyone achieves more! Associate with successful people that are in life where you want to be. Associate with other successful teachers and administrators whose schools have reached or exceeded international standards and duplicate what they have done.
- Counsel and strategize with you team leader. Set realistic personal, departmental, school, and district-level strategic plan goals, objectives, performance indicators, and action plans with your mentor and team leader.
- Read 15–20 minutes from a positive-thinking book every day just before you go to bed. (As modified and adapted for use in schools, by this author, from Jack Daughery's original 8 Essentials CORE program, Using Worldwide Dreambuilders and INA Training Models and Tools. For more information contact Tim Adsit, at 1-541-383-5119.)

Chapter 12

Foreign Languages Required

"A second language for all students is essential in an interdependent world" (*Saving America's Children*, p. 35).

"Top Ten Reasons to Learn a New Language include: 1) Communicate when you travel abroad; 2) Enhance your career; 3) Sharpen your mind; 4) Make the grade in language classes; 5) Immerse yourself in the arts, literature and more; 6) Grab the global market; 7) Explore diversity in America from Calie Ocho to Chinatown; 8) Discover new friends and ways to connect; 9) Lend a helping hand and join a global organization; 10) Improve yourself for a lifetime" (Rosetta Stone, www.bn.com/rosettastone).

FOREIGN LANGUAGES PLAY A VITAL ROLE IN AN INTERNATIONALLY COMPETITIVE SCHOOL SYSTEM

- A designated second language should be incorporated into all curricular areas, beginning in the primary years and continuing through high school graduation.
- Additional languages must be offered at the middle and high school levels.
- By sixth grade, American students should be able to listen, write, speak, and read in a second language (as adapted from *Saving America's Children*, pp. 35–36).

Chapter 13

SCANS Report on Skills Required for the Twenty-first Century—What Work Requires of Schools—Foundations for Success in the Twenty-first Century

SECRETARY'S COMMISSION ON ACHIEVING NECESSARY SKILLS (SCANS)

Background

In 1990, the Secretary of Labor appointed a commission to determine the skills our young people need to succeed in the world of work. The Commission's fundamental purpose was to encourage a high-performance economy characterized by high-skill, high-wage employment. Although the commission completed its work in 1992, its findings and recommendations continue to be a valuable source of information for individuals and organizations involved in education and work force development.

What Work Requires of Schools

The Secretary's Commission on Achieving Necessary Skills (SCANS) was asked to examine the demands of the workplace and whether today's young people are capable of meeting those demands. Specifically, the Commission was directed to advise the secretary on the level of skills required to enter employment. In carrying out this charge, the Commission was asked to:

- define the skills needed for employment;
- propose acceptable levels of proficiency;
- suggest effective ways to assess proficiency; and
- develop a dissemination strategy for the nation's schools, businesses, and homes.

This report results from the Commission's discussions and meetings with business owners, public employers, unions, and workers and supervisors in shops, plants, and stores. It builds on the work of six special panels established by the Commission to examine all manner of jobs from manufacturing to government employment. Researchers were also commissioned to conduct lengthy interviews with workers in a wide range of jobs.

Table 13.1.

SCANS Competencies	SCANS Foundation Skills
Resources	*Basic Skills*
• Allocates Time	• Reading
• Allocates Money	• Writing
• Allocates Material and Facility	• Arithmetic and Mathematics
• Resources Allocates Human Resources	• Listening
Information	• Speaking
• Acquires and Evaluates Information	*Thinking Skills*
• Organizes and Maintains Information	• Creative Thinking
• Interprets and Communicates Information	• Decision-Making
• Uses Computers to Process Information	• Problem Solving
Interpersonal	• Seeing Things in the Mind's Eye
• Participates as a Member of a Team	• Knowing How to Learn
• Teaches Others	• Reasoning
• Serves Clients/Customers	*Personal Qualities Responsibility*
• Exercises Leadership	• Self-Esteem
• Negotiates to Arrive at a Decision	• Social
• Works with Cultural Diversity	• Self-Management
Systems	• Integrity/Honesty
• Understands Systems	
• Monitors and Corrects Performance	
• Improves and Designs Systems	
Technology	
• Selects Technology	
• Applies Technology to Task	
• Maintains and Troubleshoots Technology	

SCANS

DEFINITIONS OF COMPETENCIES AND FOUNDATION SKILLS COMPETENCIES

Resources

C1 Allocates Time—Selects relevant, goal-related activities, ranks them in order of importance, allocates time to activities, and understands, prepares, and follows schedules. Competent performance in allocating time includes properly identifying tasks to be completed; ranking tasks in order of importance; developing and following an effective, workable schedule based on accurate estimates of such things as importance of tasks, time to complete tasks, time available for completion, and task deadlines; avoiding wasting time; and accurately evaluating and adjusting a schedule.

C2 Allocates Money—Uses or prepares budgets, including making cost and revenue forecasts, keeps detailed records to track budget performance, and makes appropriate adjustments. Competent performance in allocating money includes accurately preparing and using a budget according to a consistent and orderly accounting method; accurately calculating future budgetary needs based on projected costs and revenues; accurately tracking the extent to which actual costs and revenues differ from the estimated budget, and taking appropriate and effective actions.

C3 Allocates Material and Facility Resources—Acquires, stores, and distributes materials, supplies, parts, equipment, space, or final products in order to make the best use of them. Competent performance in allocating material and facility resources includes carefully planning the steps involved in the acquisition, storage, and distribution of resources; safely and efficiently acquiring, transporting or storing them; maintaining them in good condition; and distributing them to the end user.

C4 Allocates Human Resources—Assesses knowledge and skills and distributes work accordingly, evaluates performance and provides feedback. Competent performance in allocating human resources includes accurately assessing people's knowledge, skills, abilities, and potential; identifying present and future workload; making effective matches between individual talents and workload; and actively monitoring performance and providing feedback.

Information

C5 Acquires and Evaluates Information—Identifies need for data, obtains them from existing sources or creates them, and evaluates their relevance and accuracy. Competently performing the tasks of acquiring data and evaluating information includes posing analytic questions to determine specific information needs; selecting possible information and evaluating its appropriateness; and determining when new information must be created.

C6 Organizes and Maintains Information—Organizes, processes, and maintains written or computerized records and other forms of information in a systematic fashion. Competently performing the tasks of organizing and maintaining information includes understanding and organizing information from computer, visual, oral and physical sources in readily accessible formats, such as computerized data bases, spreadsheets, microfiche, video disks, paper files, and so on; when necessary, transforming data into different formats in order to organize them by the application of various methods such as sorting, classifying, or more formal methods.

C7 Interprets and Communicates Information—Selects and analyzes information and communicates the results to others using oral, written, graphic, pictorial, or multi-media methods. Competently performing the tasks of communicating and interpreting information to others includes determining information to be communicated; identifying the best methods to present information (e.g., overheads, handouts); if necessary, converting to desired format and conveying information to others through a variety of means including oral presentation, written communication, and so on.

C8 Uses Computers to Process Information—Employs computers to acquire, organize, analyze, and communicate information. Competently using computers to process information includes entering, modifying, retrieving, storing, and verifying data and other information; choosing format for display (e.g., line graphs, bar graphs, tables, pie charts, narrative); and ensuring the accurate conversion of information into the chosen format.

Interpersonal

C9 Participates as a Member of a Team—Works cooperatively with others and contributes to group with ideas, suggestions, and effort. Demonstrating competence in participating as a member of a team includes doing own share of tasks necessary to complete a project; encouraging team members by listening and responding appropriately to their contributions; building on individual team members' strengths; resolving differences for the benefit of the team; taking personal responsibility for accomplishing goals; and responsibly challenging existing procedures, policies, or authorities.

C10 Teaches Others—Helps others learn. Demonstrating competence in teaching others includes helping others to apply related concepts and theories to tasks through coaching or other means; identifying training needs; conveying job information to allow others to see its applicability and relevance to tasks; and assessing performance and providing constructive feedback/reinforcement.

C11 Serves Clients/Customers—Works and communicates with clients and customers to satisfy their expectations. Demonstrating competence in serving clients and customers includes actively listening to customers to avoid misunderstandings and identifying needs; communicating in a positive manner especially when handling complaints or conflict; efficiently obtaining additional resources to satisfy client needs.

C12 Exercises Leadership—Communicates thoughts, feelings, and ideas to justify a position, encourages, persuades, convinces, or otherwise motivates an individual or groups, including responsibly challenging existing procedures, policies, or authority. Demonstrating competence in exercising leadership includes making positive use of the rules/values followed by others; justifying a position logically and appropriately; establishing credibility through competence and integrity; and taking minority viewpoints into consideration.

C13 Negotiates to Arrive at a Decision—Works toward an agreement that may involve exchanging specific resources or resolving divergent interests. Demonstrating competence in negotiating to arrive at a decision involves researching opposition and the history of the conflict; setting realistic and attainable goals; presenting facts and arguments; listening to and reflecting on what has been said; clarifying problems and resolving conflicts; adjusting quickly to new facts/ideas; proposing and examining possible options; and making reasonable compromises.

C14 Works with Cultural Diversity—Works well with men and women and with a variety of ethnic, social, or educational backgrounds. Demonstrating competence in working with cultural diversity involves understanding one's own culture and those of others and how they differ; respecting the rights of others while helping them make cultural adjustments where necessary; basing impressions on individual performance, not on stereotypes; and understanding concerns of members of other ethnic and gender groups.

Systems

C15 Understands Systems—Knows how social, organizational, and technological systems work and operates effectively within them. Demonstrating competence in understanding systems involves knowing how a system's structures relate to goals; responding to the demands of the system/organization; knowing the right people to ask for information and where to get resources; and functioning within the formal and informal codes of the social/organizational system.

C16 Monitors and Corrects Performance—Distinguishes trends, predicts impact of actions on system operations, diagnoses deviations in the function of a system/organization, and takes necessary action to correct performance. Demonstrating competence in monitoring and correcting performance includes identifying trends and gathering needed information about how the system is intended to function; detecting deviations from system's intended purpose; troubleshooting the system; and making changes to the system to rectify system functioning and to ensure quality of product.

C17 Improves and Designs Systems—Makes suggestions to modify existing systems to improve products or services and develops new or alterative systems. Demonstrating competence in improving or designing systems involves making suggestions for improving the functioning of the system or organization; recommending alterative system designs based on relevant feedback; and responsibly challenging the status quo to benefit the larger system.

Technology

C18 Selects Technology—Judges which set of procedures, tools, or machines, including computers and their programs, will produce the desired results. Demonstrating competence in selecting technology includes determining desired outcomes and applicable constraints; visualizing the necessary methods and applicable technology; evaluating specifications; and judging which machine or tool will produce the desired results.

C19 Applies Technology to Task—Understands the overall intent and the proper procedures for setting up and operating machines, including computers and their programming systems. Demonstrating competence in how to apply technology to task includes understanding how different parts of machines interact and how machines interact with broader production systems; on occasion installing machines including computers; setting up machines or systems of machines efficiently to get desired results; accurately interpreting machine output; and detecting errors from program output.

C20 Maintains and Troubleshoots Technology—Prevents, identifies, or solves problems in machines, computers, and other technologies. Demonstrating competence in maintaining and troubleshooting technology includes identifying, understanding, and performing routine preventative maintenance and service on technology; detecting more serious problems; generating workable solutions to correct deviations; and recognizing when to get additional help.

FOUNDATION SKILLS

Basic Skills

F1 Reading—Locates, understands, and interprets written information in prose and documents—including manuals, graphs, and schedules—to perform tasks; learns from text by determining the main idea or essential message; identifies relevant details, facts, and specifications; infers or locates the meaning of unknown or technical vocabulary; and judges the accuracy, appropriateness, style, and plausibility of reports, proposals, or theories of other writers.

F2 Writing—Communicates thoughts, ideas, information, and messages in writing; records information completely and accurately; composes and creates documents such as letters, directions, manuals, reports, proposals, graphs, flow-charts; uses language, style, organization, and format appropriate to the subject matter, purpose, and audience; includes supporting documentation and attends to level of detail; and checks, edits, and revises for correct information, appropriate emphasis, form, grammar, spelling, and punctuation.

F3 Arithmetic—Performs basic computations; uses basic numerical concepts such as whole numbers and percentages in practical situations; makes reasonable estimates of arithmetic results without a calculator; and uses tables, graphs, diagrams, and charts to obtain or convey quantitative information.

F4 Mathematics—Approaches practical problems by choosing appropriately from a variety of mathematical techniques; uses quantitative data to construct logical explanations for real world situations; expresses mathematical ideas and concepts orally and in writing; and understands the role of chance in the occurrence and prediction of events. [This skill definition is not yet completely developed.]

F5 Listening—Receives, attends to, interprets, and responds to verbal messages and other cues such as body language in ways that are appropriate to the purpose; for example, to comprehend, to learn, to critically evaluate, to appreciate, or to support the speaker.

F6 Speaking—Organizes ideas and communicates oral messages appropriate to listeners and situations; participates in conversation, discussion, and group presentations; selects an appropriate medium for conveying a message; uses verbal language and other cues such as body language appropriate in style, tone, and level of complexity to the audience and the occasion; speaks clearly and communicates a message; understands and responds to listener feedback; and asks questions when needed.

F7 Creative Thinking—Uses imagination freely, combines ideas or information in new ways, makes connections between seemingly unrelated ideas, and reshapes goals in ways that reveal new possibilities.

F8 Decision Making—Specifies goals and constraints, generates alternatives, considers risks, and evaluates and chooses best alternative.

F9 Problem Solving—Recognizes that a problem exists (i.e., there is a discrepancy between what is and what should or could be); identifies possible reasons for the discrepancy; devises and implements a plan of action to resolve it; evaluates and monitors progress; and revises plan as indicated by findings.

F10 Seeing Things in the Mind's Eye—Organizes and processes symbols, pictures, graphs, objects or other information; for example, sees a building from a blueprint, a system's operation from schematics, the flow of work activities from narrative descriptions, or the taste of food from reading a recipe.

F11 Knowing How to Learn—Recognizes and can use learning techniques to apply and adapt new knowledge and skills in both familiar and changing situations and is aware of teaming tools such as personal teaming styles (visual, aural, etc.), formal learning strategies (note taking or clustering items that share some characteristics), and informal teaming strategies (awareness of unidentified false assumptions that may lead to faulty conclusions). [This skill definition is not yet completely developed.]

F12 Reasoning—Discovers a rule or principle underlying the relationship between two or more objects and applies it in solving a problem;

uses logic to draw conclusions from available information; extracts rules or principles from a set of objects or written text; applies rules and principles to a new situation or determines which conclusions are correct when given a set of facts and a set of conclusions. [This skill definition is not yet completely developed.]

Personal Qualities

F13 Responsibility—Exerts a high level of effort and perseverance toward goal attainment; works hard to become excellent at doing tasks by setting high standards, paying attention to details, working well and displaying a high level of concentration even when assigned an unpleasant task; and displays high standards of attendance, punctuality, enthusiasm, vitality, and optimism in approaching and completing tasks.

F14 Self-Esteem—Believes in own self-worth and maintains a positive view of self; demonstrates knowledge of own skills and abilities; is aware of impact on others; and knows own emotional capacity and needs and how to address them. [This skill definition is not yet completely developed.]

F15 Social—Demonstrates understanding, friendliness, adaptability, empathy and politeness in new and on-going group settings; asserts self in familiar and unfamiliar social situations; relates well to others; responds appropriately as the situation requires; and takes an interest in what others say and do.

F16 Self-Management—Assesses own knowledge, skills, and abilities accurately; sets well-defined and realistic personal goals; monitors progress toward goal attainment and motivates self through goal achievement; exhibits self-control and responds to feedback unemotionally and non-defensively; and is a "self-starter."

F17 Integrity/Honesty—Can be trusted; recognizes when faced with making a decision or exhibiting behavior that may break with commonly-held personal or societal values; understands the impact of violating these beliefs and codes on an organization, self, and others; and chooses an ethical course of action. [This skill definition is not yet completely developed.]

(These extended excerpts are from the book *Skills and Tasks for Jobs: A SCANS Report for America 2000* published by the U.S. Department of Labor. The book may be purchased from the U.S. Government Printing Office under ISBN 0-16-036177-X.)

Bibliographic data below was posted to EdNet by Mr. Thomas J. Pitre, whose e-mail account appears to be with the California State University System. The data itself is from the University of Saskatchewan Library System: ED350414.

Foundations for Success in the Twenty-first Century

"Success is the progressive realization of a worthwhile goal or dream that is not against God's laws or man's laws" (Ron Puryear, speech given in a Worldwide Dream Builder function held at the Portland Coliseum, 8:00 p.m., Portland, OR, 1980).

WORKPLACE KNOW-HOW

The know-how identified by SCANS is made up of *five competencies* and a *three-part foundation of skills and personal qualities* that are needed for solid job performance.

Competencies

Effective workers can productively use:

- *Resources*—allocating time, money, materials, space, and staff;
- *Interpersonal Skills*—working on teams, teaching others, serving customers, leading, negotiating, and working well with people from culturally diverse backgrounds;
- *Information*—acquiring and evaluating data, organizing and maintaining files, interpreting and communicating, and using computers to process information;
- *Systems*—understanding social, organizational, and technological systems, monitoring and correcting performance, and designing or improving systems;
- *Technology*—selecting equipment and tools, applying technology to specific tasks, and maintaining and troubleshooting technologies.

Competencies differ from a person's technical knowledge. For example, both accountants and engineers manage resources, information, systems, and technology. They require competence in these areas even though building a bridge has little to do with balancing a set of books.

The Foundation

Competence requires:

- *Basic Skills*—reading, writing, arithmetic and mathematics, speaking and listening;
- *Thinking Skills*—thinking creatively, making decisions, solving problems, seeing things in the mind's eye, knowing how to learn, and reasoning;
- *Personal Qualities*—individual responsibility, self-esteem, sociability, self-management, and integrity.

FIVE COMPETENCIES (EXPANDED)

1. *Resources:* Identifies, organizes, plans, and allocates resources
   a. Time—selects goal-relevant activities, ranks them, allocates time, and prepares and follows schedules
   b. Money—uses or prepares budgets, makes forecasts, keeps records, and makes adjustments to meet objectives
   c. Materials and Facilities—acquires, stores, allocates, and uses materials or space efficiently
   d. Human Resources—assesses skills and distributes work accordingly, evaluates performance and provides feedback

2. *Interpersonal:* Works with others
   a. Participates as Member of a Team—contributes to group effort
   b. Teaches Others New Skills
   c. Serves Clients/Customers—works to satisfy customers' expectations
   d. Exercises Leadership—communicates ideas to justify position, persuades and convinces others, responsibly challenges existing procedures and policies
   e. Negotiates—works toward agreements involving exchange of resources, resolves divergent interests
   f. Works with Diversity—works well with men and women from diverse backgrounds

3. *Information:* Acquires and uses information
   a. Acquires and Evaluates Information
   b. Organizes and Maintains Information
   c. Interprets and Communicates Information
   d. Uses Computers to Process Information

4. *Systems:* Understands complex inter-relationships
   a. Understands Systems—knows how social, organizational, and technological systems work and operates effectively with them
   b. Monitors and Corrects Performance—distinguishes trends, predicts impacts on system operations, diagnoses deviations in systems' performance and corrects malfunctions
   c. Improves or Designs Systems—suggests modifications to existing systems and develops new or alternative systems to improve performance

5. *Technology:* Works with a variety of technologies
   a. Selects Technology—chooses procedures, tools or equipment including computers and related technologies
   b. Applies Technology to Task—understands overall intent and proper procedures for setup and operation of equipment
   c. Maintains and Troubleshoots Equipment—prevents, identifies, or solves problems with equipment, including computers and other technologies

A THREE-PART FOUNDATION

1. *Basic Skills:* Reads, writes, performs arithmetic and mathematical operations, listens and speaks
   a. Reading—locates, understands, and interprets written information in prose and in documents such as manuals, graphs, and schedules
   b. Writing—communicates thoughts, ideas, information, and messages in writing; creates documents such as letters, directions, manuals, reports, graphs, and flow charts
   c. Arithmetic-Mathematics—performs basic computations and approaches practical problems by choosing appropriately from a variety of mathematical techniques
   d. Listening—receives, attends to, interprets, and responds to verbal messages and other clues
   e. Speaking—organizes ideas and communicates orally

2. *Thinking Skills:* Thinks creatively, makes decisions, solves problems, visualizes, knows how to learn, and reasons
   a. Creative Thinking—generates new ideas
   b. Decision-Making—specifies goals and constraints, generates alternatives, considers risks, and evaluates and chooses best alternative
   c. Problem Solving—recognizes problems and devises and implements plan of action

d. Seeing Things in the Mind's Eye—organizes and processes symbols, pictures, graphs, objects and other information
e. Knowing How to Learn—uses efficient learning techniques to acquire and apply new knowledge and skills
f. Reasoning—discovers a rule or principle underlying the relationship between two or more objects and applies it when solving a problem

3. *Personal Qualities:* Displays responsibility, self-esteem, sociability, self-management, and integrity
    a. Responsibility—exerts a high level of effort and perseveres toward goal attainment
    b. Self-Esteem—believes in own self-worth and maintains a positive view of self
    c. Sociability—demonstrates understanding, friendliness, adaptability, empathy, and politeness in group settings
    d. Self-Management—assesses self accurately, sets personal goals, monitors progress, and exhibits self-control
    e. Integrity/Honesty—chooses ethical courses of action

Work involves a complex interplay among the five competencies, higher-order thinking skills, and diligent application of personal qualities.

SCANS RELATIONSHIP TO NATIONAL GOALS

- *Goal #3:* American students will leave grades 4, 8, and 12 having demonstrated competency in challenging subject matter, including English, mathematics, science, history, and geography; and every school in America will ensure that all students learn to use their minds well, so they may be prepared for responsible citizenship, further learning, and productive employment in our modern economy.
- *Goal #5:* Every adult American will be literate and will possess the knowledge and skills necessary to compete in a global economy and exercise the rights and responsibilities of citizenship.

**The information in the preceding sections, as well as what is shown in the tables 13.2 and 13.3, is taken from "Competing in the New International Economy," Washington, DC: Office of Technology Assessment, 1990; posted to the Internet August 14, 1996, at http://www.uni.edu/darrow/frames/scans.html.

Table 13.2. Levels of Progress in Acquiring Skills

Proficiency Level	Performance Benchmark
Preparatory	Scheduling oneself
Work-Ready	Scheduling small work team
Intermediate	Scheduling a production line or substantial construction project
Advanced	Developing roll-out schedule for new product or production plant
Specialist	Develop algorithm for scheduling airline

Table 13.3. Characteristics of Today's and Tomorrow's Workplace

TRADITIONAL MODEL	HIGH PERFORMANCE MODEL
STRATEGY: PRODUCTION	
mass production	flexible production
long production runs	customized production
centralized control	decentralized control
STRATEGY: QUALITY CONTROL	
fixed automation	flexible automation
end-of-line quality control	on-line quality control
fragmentation of tasks	work teams, multi-skilled workers
authority vested in supervisor	authority delegated to worker
STRATEGY: HIRING AND HUMAN RESOURCES	
labor-management confrontation	labor-management cooperation
minimal qualifications accepted	screening for basic skills abilities
workers as a cost	work force as an investment
STRATEGY: JOB LADDERS	
internal labor market	limited internal labor market
advancement by seniority	advancement by certified skills
STRATEGY: TRAINING	
minimal for production workers	training sessions for everyone
specialized for craft workers	broader skills sought

Source: "Competing in the New International Economy." Washington, D.C.: Office of Technology Assessment, 1990.

GLOSSARY OF TERMS

Basic Skills

Reading

Locates, understands, and interprets written information in prose and documents—including manuals, graphs, and schedules—to perform tasks; learns from text by determining the main idea or essential message; identifies relevant details, facts, and specifications; infers or locates the meaning of unknown or technical vocabulary; and judges the accuracy, appropriateness, style, and plausibility of reports, proposals, or theories of other writers.

Writing

Communicates thoughts, ideas, information, and messages in writing; records information completely and accurately; composes and creates documents such as letters, directions, manuals, reports, proposals, graphs, flow charts; uses language, style, organization, and format appropriate to the subject matter, purpose, and audience. Includes supporting documentation and attends to level of detail; checks, edits, and revises for correct information, appropriate emphasis, form, grammar, spelling, and punctuation.

Arithmetic/Mathematics

Arithmetic—Performs basic computations; uses basic numerical concepts such as whole numbers and percentages in practical situations; makes reasonable estimates of arithmetic results without a calculator; and uses tables, graphs, diagrams, and charts to obtain or convey quantitative information.

Mathematics—Approaches practical problems by choosing appropriately from a variety of mathematical techniques; uses quantitative data to construct logical explanations for real world situations; expresses mathematical ideas and concepts orally and in writing; and understands the role of chance in the occurrence and prediction of events.

Listening

Receives, attends to, interprets, and responds to verbal messages and other cues such as body language in ways that are appropriate to the purpose; for example, to comprehend; to learn; to critically evaluate; to appreciate; or to support the speaker.

Speaking

Organizes ideas and communicates oral messages appropriate to listeners and situations; participates in conversation, discussion, and group presentations; selects an appropriate medium for conveying a message; uses verbal languages and other cues such as body language appropriate in style, tone, and level of complexity to the audience and the occasion; speaks clearly and communicates message; understands and responds to listener feed back; and asks questions when needed.

Thinking Skills

Creative Thinking

Uses imagination freely, combines ideas or information in new ways, makes connections between seemingly unrelated ideas, and reshapes goals in ways that reveal new possibilities.

Decision-Making

Specifies goals and constraints, generates alternatives, considers risks, and evaluates and chooses best alternatives.

Problem Solving

Recognizes that a problem exists (i.e., there is a discrepancy between what is and what should or could be), identifies possible reasons for the discrepancy, and devises and implements a plan of action to resolve it. Evaluates and monitors progress, and revises plan as indicated by findings.

Seeing Things in the Mind's Eye

Organizes and processes symbols, pictures, graphs, objects or other information; for example, see a building from blue print, a system's operation from schematics, the flow of work activities from narrative descriptions, or the taste of food from reading a recipe.

Knowing How to Learn

Recognizes and can use learning techniques to apply and adapt new knowledge and skills in both familiar and changing situations. Involves being aware of learning tools such as personal learning styles (visual, aural, etc.), formal learning strategies (note taking or clustering items that share some characteristics), and informal learning strategies (awareness of unidentified false assumptions that may lead to faulty conclusions).

Reasoning

Discovers a rule or principle underlying the relationship between two or more objects and applies it in solving a problem. For example, uses logic to draw conclusions from available information, extracts rules or principles from a set of objects or written text; applies rules and principles to a new situation, or determines which conclusions are correct when given a set of facts and a set of conclusions.

Personal Qualities

Responsibility

Exerts a high level of effort and perseverance towards goal attainment. Works hard to become excellent at doing tasks by setting high standards, paying attention to details, working well, and displaying a high level concentration even when assigned an unpleasant task. Displays high standards of attendance, punctuality, enthusiasm, vitality, and optimism in approaching and completing tasks.

Self-Esteem

Believes in own self-worth and maintains a positive view of self; demonstrates knowledge of own skills and abilities; is aware of impact on others; and knows own emotional capacity and needs and how to address them.

Sociability

Demonstrates understanding, friendliness, adaptability, empathy, and politeness in new and on-going group settings. Asserts self in familiar and unfamiliar social situations; relates well to others; responds appropriately as the situation requires; and takes an interest in what others say and do.

Self-Management

Assesses own knowledge, skills, and abilities accurately; sets well-defined and realistic personal goals; monitors progress toward goal attainment and motivates self through goal achievement; exhibits self-control and responds to feedback unemotionally and nondefensively; is a "self-starter."

Integrity/Honesty

Can be trusted. Recognizes when faced with making a decision or exhibiting behavior that may break with commonly-held personal or societal values; understands the impact of violating these beliefs and codes on an organizations, self, and others; and chooses an ethical course of action.

**Taken from *What Work Requires of Schools: A SCANS Report for America 2000*, June 1991.

Chapter 14

Two-Year Action Plan To Reach National Education Standards

"To accomplish your goals and be a success in this or any endeavor do four things: (1) Decide what you want; (2) Decide what you are willing to give up to get what you want, (3) Plan your work, and (4) Work your plan consistently and persistently."

—Dave Severn

- *Year 1: A New Beginning*
- *Step 1—Community Awareness*
- *Step 2—Community Consensus on New School Purpose and Goals*
- *Step 3—Community Consensus on Needed Academic Skills and Knowledge*
- *Step 4—Negotiables and Non-Negotiables*
  - *May require collective bargaining where necessary at either local or national level*
- *Step 5—Develop a Strategic Action Plan for Implementation*
- *Year 2: Implementation*

The following detailed two-year plan for reaching national education standards was originally from *Partners For Success: Business and Education*, which appeared in a book and video describing the work of a respected group of school principals who guided underachieving schools to nationally recognized academic success. This plan was reproduced in the report entitled *Saving America's Children: Achieving International Standards in American Schools—A Blueprint for Change* and is reprinted here with written permission.

YEAR 1

Month 1

Assess Strengths and Needs

Elicit assistance of staff and parents to collect and collate hard-core data:

- (Implement time management forms. You will need to manage your time very carefully and stay focused on reaching national standards in two years.)
- History of students' achievement levels
- Current test results
- Attendance and suspension patterns
- Instructional materials
- Homework procedures, policies, and current practices
- Condition of the physical plant including safety and appearance
- Discipline and behavior
- Existing rules and standards
- Communication with staff, students, and parents
- Quality and quantity of parent and student involvement with the school
- Student and staff population

Analyze the Curriculum and Instruction

- State and local mandates
- Existing program design
- Implementation, monitoring, and evaluation systems
- Staff development
- Staff evaluation

High expectations are publicized from the beginning. Excuses for failure are systematically buried with the trash.

Internalize Effective School Practices

- Study effective schools' research (as cited elsewhere in this book)
- Observe an effective school(s) personally
- Network with other successful principals, teachers, and parents
- Identify teachers and practices that currently demonstrate effective practices and reward publicly in staff meetings, or before parent groups, and in the community.

The stage is (now) set for high expectations beginning with the principal. All staff know what the norm should be measured by.

Month 2

Establishing a philosophy is essential. Communicate a vision to staff, students, and parents of academic success for all students.

Form a Core Leadership Team

The leadership team should reflect race, gender, job classification, and grade levels of the school, including:

- Administration
- Staff
- Parents
- Union representatives

Develop a School Profile Based on Hard-Core Data

- Profile of students' achievements—collectively and individually
- Profile of staff
- Profile of the community
- Description of the school's strengths and weaknesses

Develop a Mission Statement

Based on the school profile, develop the mission statement into an action plan for the year. Plans should be prepared for each, including:

- Curriculum
- Performance objectives
- Staff development
- Evaluation process
- Support
- Design and organize appropriate handbooks

The author suggests using a Strategic Action Planning Form with the following headings for implementation of this plan:

- Goal
- Objectives
- Priority

- Action Tasks
- Due Date
- Responsible Person
- Results/Progress to Date/Percent Complete/Dependencies
- Comments

It may be necessary for the principal to dictate some major changes quickly (i.e., facility repair and student discipline). These immediate successes can be used as a springboard for future, more abstract changes.

Month 3

Publicize Openly—the Good News, the Bad News, and Plans for Improvement

- Orient all teachers and staff
- Communicate clear expectations
- Develop lesson and unit plans to meet goals (using Madeline Hunter's 7-step lesson design presented by this author elsewhere in this book)
- Implement the support plan

Begin Ongoing Staff Development and Monitor Progress Regularly

Be in every classroom every day. (Manage by walking around.) Ask teachers three simple questions: What are you doing? How does it relate to what you did yesterday? How does it relate to what you will do tomorrow (to reach national standards)?

Begin the Evaluation and Assessment Process

Months 4–5

Review and monitor student achievement by school, grade, class, and individual

Months 6–7

- Continue implementation plans
- Continue staff development
- Publicly recognize successes
- Conduct frequent monitoring and committee meetings (team meetings, departmental or grade-level meetings, school site council meetings, core team meetings)

Month 8

- Refine long-range plans and make appropriate changes

Month 9

- Plan appropriate standardized testing procedures
- Monitor progress

Months 10–11

- Monitor implementation of testing
- Monitor end-of-year activities
- Develop a new, complete school profile

Month 12

- Reassess programs and priorities
- Adjust school plan for next year
- Involve staff in professional development programs based on school profile and assessment of needs (Conducted prior to leaving for summer; design summer in-service activities and activities for year 2 based on this needs assessment after year 1. Preferably, master teachers from your own building, another building in your district, or from a close neighboring district will teach peers in these staff development activities. If not, teach them yourself, if you are able, or ask your local ESD or Boces or your State Department of Education to provide master teachers who will design training specifically for the needs identified in your building and/or district. If possible, pay teachers a professional stipend for attending summer training and/or allow for in-district credit and movement on the salary schedule as an incentive for professional, certified staff and instructional, classified support staff attendance.) (parenthesis mine, added through years of practical experience implementing this plan)

YEAR 2

Begin again, building on previous success and addressing remaining needs and/or concerns using Shirley Hord's Concerns-Based Adoption Model described in her book entitled *Taking Charge of Change*, presented elsewhere in this book.

- Restate mission of school frequently (to continuously improve student learning and achievement to meet or exceed national standards in 2 years)
- Re-emphasize high expectations of performance by staff and students
- Involve staff and parents in problem solving and decision-making
- Publicize results of performance, and climb toward (new national) goals
- Reward success and (celebrate success) often
- Monitor progress and performance of all areas regularly
- Study and internalize effective schools' research (mentioned elsewhere in this book)
- Identify what the international standards are that you will continue to work towards in the next two years following this one
- Network with other successful schools (who have reached national standards and who have either reached or exceeded international standards and send a visitation team to review their program, etc.)

Chapter 15

Two-Year Action Plan To Reach International Standards

"There is no such thing such thing as a goal too big, only a flexible accomplishment date."

—Dave Severns

"There are seven sequential steps requisite to setting and implementing well-defined goals and objectives: (1) Diagnosing the Problem; (2) Formulating Goals and Objectives; (3) Identifying Constraints and Needed Resources; (4) Evaluating Alternatives; (5) Selecting Solutions; (6) Implementing the Selected Solutions; and (7) Feedback and Evaluation."

—Richard W. Hostrop, *Managing Education for Results*, p. 62

REACHING INTERNATIONAL STANDARDS

Implementing strategies to raise our children's academic achievement to international standards will not be an accident. The following strategies for implementation will guarantee students the skills and abilities needed to succeed in the twenty-first century and also foster a positive attitude toward lifelong learning.

Year 1: A New Beginning

Step 1. Community Awareness (3 to 6 months)

Successful educators, astute parents, and informed business people know our education system is facing a state of emergency. Although the American public seems to be voicing agreement, few communities will admit that there is anything wrong with their school.

It is absolutely imperative that local schools plan a detailed awareness campaign to inform internal and external community members of the need for change—and the eventual cost of not changing.

Specific international statistics, business needs, and governmental information must be disseminated. We suggest that students be a primary audience and be taught to ask, "Why am I learning this?"

- Designate one individual or department to gather information regarding effective schools and international techniques and standards.
- Compile relevant school profile data and make evaluative comparisons for students within the district.
- List strengths and weaknesses and candidly report to internal and external publics.
- Prepare five distinct reports aimed at five audiences (educators, business, parents, community, students, and, I would add, board) that detail where you are and where you need to be.
- Present reports to all groups and recruit resources (both human and nonhuman).
- With this select group, plan an in-depth awareness campaign for the community at large.
- Publicize results of the awareness campaign and decide whether to continue. (I found that continuous, year-round communications campaigns are the most effective. Tell them, tell them what you told them, and tell them again!)

Step 2. Community Consensus on New School Purpose and Goals (3–6 Months)

"The American public and education community do not know the purpose of elementary and secondary education anymore. When we talk about what we are going to teach and assess in our schools, it is based upon our institutional heritage and what were taught. It is not based upon a systematic analysis of what children are going to use in their adult years (in the twenty-first century). A detailed plan of what skills and knowledge students need is necessary" (Dr. Willard Daggett, *Saving America's Children*, 1992, p. 38).

- Create a group of influential community members composed of the five original target groups to outline specifically the purpose of your school (as opposed to the vision and the mission).

- Initiate any and all strategies necessary to compile this information for a community consensus.
- Publicize your community's next steps.

Step 3. Community Consensus on Needed Academic Skills and Knowledge (4 Months)

Once a systematic analysis has led to the development of school purpose and goals, consensus must next be reached on what skills and knowledge students must have to reach the stated goals. (Detailed earlier in this document; see pages 1–36 of the 1992 *Saving America's Children* report mentioned previously in this book. See also the SCANS Report included in chapter 13 of this book.)

The institutional setting that currently governs our delivery of instruction cannot be allowed to prevent us from reaching high levels of education.

- Specifically identify the knowledge, skills, and attitudes that need to be learned to match the goals of the school. This must be done for both school staff and students.
- Identify how staff will acquire new skills, or how new instruction will be made available to students, possibly using distance-learning technologies.
- Disregard all instructional restraints when making your plans.
- Aim to exceed international standards at all levels.

Step 4. Negotiables and Non-Negotiables (1 Month)

"In American education, it is okay to reform schools as long as you do not affect an adult role. This relegates us to no real change.

"School systems need to confront all institutional roles and decide which are negotiable and which are not. If the school year needs lengthening, will the public agree to fund the change or will educators agree to work for less?

"Does the sanctity of subject-centered course work override the identified need for an interdisciplinary approach to education if it means the elimination of administrators and teachers?

"Communities need to confront each obstacle and agree on which are negotiable, and which are not, before real change can be implemented" (Dr. Willard Daggett, *Saving America's Children*, 1992, p. 39).

- Courageously confront every obstacle that impedes essential skill attainment and determine whether or not the institutional structure will negotiate change.

- Get specific, guaranteed commitments from government, labor, business, and management for each institutional change negotiated.
- Get specific, signed policy statements from any party that refuses to negotiate on an item that is deemed essential.
- Create a mechanism that allows for immediate change and flexibility should new areas or situations occur that are open for negotiation.

Step 5. Develop a Plan For Implementation (2 Months)

The four steps previously listed must be completed before this step can be attempted. There is no mystery to writing a plan. Those interested in change will do so swiftly.

- Use successful practices that are common to the area for planning strategies.
- Determine costs and secure committed funding and resources.
- Continually report to all areas of the community and publicize final plan with time lines (who is responsible), and accountability checks in place.

Year 2: Implementation

Implementing your completed plan will be the easiest step in the process for real change. Curricula need to be rewritten, new assessment techniques developed, and teachers need to be retrained. (Please review pages 1–36 in *Saving America's Children*, 1992, carefully to ensure that you have covered all the bases.)

The work will be difficult, but we have the resources available to make these changes happen rather quickly. We submit that past implementation plans and schemes failed to work because little effort has been put into achieving the first four steps described in this process.

- Follow the plan.
- Begin the second school year implementing changes that raise achievement to international standards.
- Monitor the plan and revise when necessary.
- Along the way, celebrate successes with your community.

This plan was reproduced in the report entitled *Saving America's Children: Achieving International Standards in American Schools—A Blueprint for Change* as presented by Associated Oregon Industries and the National Association for Schools of Excellence, 1992, and is reprinted here by written permission.

Chapter 16

The Founding Fathers' Beliefs on Leadership

"When the competition thinks you're down for the count, you have an opportunity to achieve a major victory. March while the competition is sleeping . . . ride to the front and motion for the troops to follow. Rest when necessary, but stay close to the competition so as to keep a watchful eye on their actions."

—Donald T. Phillips, *The Founding Fathers on Leadership*

"A Servant's Heart . . . becoming excited about making someone else successful."

—John 5:12–13

"Leadership . . . seeing the consequences of our actions further in the future than those around us can."

—1 Thessalonians 5:12–14

"Achievement . . . helping a person find out what he needs then helping him find the best way to get it."

—1 Thessalonians 2:11

"Above all things I hope the education of the common people will be attended to; convinced that on their good sense we may rely with the most security for the preservation of a due degree of liberty."

—James Madison, December 20, 1787

Chapter 16

"Knowledge is power, Knowledge is safety, and Knowledge is happiness."

—Thomas Jefferson to George Ticknor, November 25, 1817

"It is impossible to rightly govern a nation without God and the Bible."

—George Washington

"The only thing more expensive than education is ignorance."

"Tell me and I forget. Teach me and I remember. Involve me and I learn."

"By failing to prepare, you are preparing to fail."

"An investment in knowledge always pays the best interest."

"For having lived long, I have experienced many instances of being obliged, by better information or fuller consideration, to change opinions, even on important subjects, which I once thought right but found to be otherwise."

"Without continual growth and progress, such words as improvement, achievement, and success have no meaning."

—Ben Franklin

"Wise statesman as they were, they knew the tendency of prosperity to breed tyrants, and so they established these great self-evident truths, that when in the distant future some man, some faction, some interest, should set up the doctrine that none but rich men, or none but white men, were entitled to life, liberty and the pursuit of happiness, their posterity might look up again to the Declaration of Independence . . . so that truth, and justice, and mercy, and all the humane and Christian virtues might not be extinguished from the land."

—Abraham Lincoln on the founding fathers, August 17, 1858

The reader is referred to Donald T. Phillips, *Founding Fathers on Leadership: Classic Teamwork in Changing Times*, 1997. The following comes from that source:

Part I/Preparing for the Revolution

1/Sound the Trumpet
2/Create a Vision, Set Goals, and Involve Everyone
3/Build Your Team and Be Decisive (No Decision Constipation)
4/Inspire the Masses

Part II/Mobilizing and Motivating

5/First Listen, Then Communicate
6/Travel with the Troops
7/Turn a Negative into a Positive
8/Harass, Innovate, and Leverage Resources

Part III/Winning the War

9/Build Strong Alliances (and Coalitions)
10/Attend to Financial Matters
11/Refuse to Lose and Learn Continuously
12/Be a Risk-Taker

Part IV/After the Revolution

13/Understand Human Nature
14/Compromise and Create the Culture
15/Stick Around and Follow Through (Develop Future Leaders and Pass The Torch To The Next Generation)

Chapter 17

What Works in Education: A Research Synthesis

Abstract writers from ERIC state:

> Educational research studies conducted in recent years are distilled into 59 significant findings or conclusions that can be used as a practical guide for parents and teachers seeking those educational practices found to be most effective in helping children to learn. The 59 findings are displayed one to a page. Each page is organized into three parts: (1) the "research finding," stated succinctly; (2) several paragraphs of "comment" elaborating on the finding; and (3) "references" to the major educational research studies that support the finding. The findings cover such topics as: reading to children, counting, early writing, developing talent, getting parents involved, phonics, science experiments, managing classroom time, tutoring, memorization, homework, school climate, discipline, effective principals, cultural literacy, foreign language, rigorous courses, extracurricular activities, and preparation for work. The 59 findings are grouped under three major headings: Home (9 topics), Classroom (29 topics), and School (21 topics).
>
> This handbook represents a concerted effort to demonstrate that the educational process is susceptible to being understood and that research can reveal practical concepts that will improve that process. It is an attempt to supply clear, accurate, reliable, and non-controversial information to parents and educators on some of the most important everyday educational questions. The original "What Works" (March 1986) contained 41 selected research findings about what works when it comes to educating a child. This updated edition contains an additional 19 findings, covering such topics as: television, teacher feedback, behavior problems, illustrations, solving word problems, cooperative learning, reading aloud, character education, libraries, attendance, success in a new school, mainstreaming, school to work transition. One earlier finding, on unexcused absences, was dropped (*What Works: Research about Teaching and Learning*, second edition, 1987).

WHAT WORKS IN THE CLASSROOM:
The McREL Report in a Nutshell

Likewise, reviewers from Education Up Close state, "For years, the U.S. Department of Education has been investing heavily in educational research designed to investigate everything from equity to violence prevention. Usually their work results in encyclopedic tomes about the state of education and the implementation of lofty educational goals. This is important research, to be sure, but you may wonder, how does it help the teachers in the trenches?

"Fortunately for teachers and students alike, the Mid-continent Research for Education and Learning (McREL) has recently published a practical guide to teaching strategies that work called *What Works in Classroom Instruction*.

"As you probably guessed, this manual is no thin pamphlet you'll tuck into your back pocket. It weighs in at nearly two hundred pages. Thankfully, McREL has wisely posted it online in portable-document format (PDF) so that busy teachers and administrators can access it easily and often.

"The McREL guide stands out because it is not only based on hard scientific research, but just as importantly, it actually shows teachers how to use effective teaching strategies in the classroom.

McREL Follows-Up on Reagan-Era Challenge

"In an unprecedented effort, McREL followed-up on a challenge made in 1986 from then-Secretary of Education William J. Bennett to synthesize the research in education so that it can be made useful to the American public.

"In response, authors Robert J. Marzano, Barbara B. Gaddy, and Ceri Dean set out to 'Provide educators with instructional strategies that research shows have the greatest likelihood of positively affecting student learning.'

Strategies as Tools

"Amid their efforts to distill hundreds of research studies into what is, essentially, a short list of teaching strategies, one persistent point emerged: strategies are merely tools. The authors found that no one strategy works under all conditions, with all levels of student achievement or teaching expertise. The teacher must always consider the context of the educational situation when applying any one of the teaching strategies McREL recommends.

Nine Instructional Strategies Identified

"*What Works in Classroom Instruction* outlines nine basic classroom strategies that have been shown to work. If you have done any professional development in the past five years, you will be pleasantly surprised to find that the strategies reflect current models of best practices. The strategies are usable to educators who subscribe to a wide variety of divergent theories and frameworks on human learning and cognition. In other words, regardless of whether you believe in multiple intelligences or some other theory, you should be able to use these in your classroom.

"*The Nine Instructional Strategies in a Nutshell*

1. Identifying Similarities and Differences
2. Summarizing and Note Taking
3. Reinforcing Effort and Providing Recognition
4. Homework and Practice
5. Nonlinguistic Representations
6. Cooperative Learning
7. Setting Goals and Providing Feedback
8. Generating and Testing Hypotheses
9. Activating Prior Knowledge

"The manual provides detailed discussions of each strategy in a straightforward manner. At the onset of each chapter, the guide describes an example of the strategy in use. It then goes on to discuss the theory and research behind it and concludes with more illustrations and ideas for using the strategy. Following each strategy description is a discussion of the how it can be used to develop five types of knowledge: vocabulary, details, organizing ideas, skills, and processes. The last chapter demonstrates how a teacher might incorporate them all into a cohesive unit of instruction. Regardless of the subject you teach or where you are in your teaching career, *What Works in Classroom Instruction* will give you plenty of ideas to incorporate effective teaching strategies into your practice.

Finding the Report

"To read *What Works in Classroom Instruction* by Robert J. Marzano, Barbara B. Gaddy, and Ceri Dean en toto, go to the McREL web site. There you can either read it online, print the report out on your own printer (it's 173 pages), or order a copy from their Web site for $25.00" (Education Up Close, August 2006).

Chapter 18

Effective Schooling Practices

Too voluminous to include in its entirety here, "The effective schooling research base identifies schooling practices and characteristics associated with measurable improvements in student achievement and excellence in student behavior. These 'effective schooling practices' include elements of schooling associated with a clearly defined curriculum; focused classroom instruction and management; firm, consistent discipline; close monitoring of student performance and strong instructional leadership."

(For further information or to obtain a copy, ask for Dr. Robert E. Blum, *Effective Schooling Practices: A Research Synthesis—Onward to Excellence: Making Schools More Effective* (1984), Education Northwest, 101 SW Main St, Ste 500, Portland, OR 97204-3213; Phone: (503) 275-9500; Fax: (503) 275-0660; educationnorthwest.org/contact.)

Chapter 19

What Makes Some Schools and Teachers More Effective?

Many years ago, in 1981 to be exact, Dr. Richard H. Hersh, then associate provost of research at the University of Oregon, originally presented the material that follows at the Oregon School Study Council sponsored breakfast during the Oregon School Boards Association's 1981 annual convention, in Portland, Oregon. His study of the literature was funded by a National Institute of Education contract with the Center for Educational Policy and Management at the University of Oregon, where this author took certification courses for becoming a superintendent and principal, and did work towards a Ph.D. degree in Educational Administration. I was serving Harrisburg Union High School District as their superintendent and high school principal at the time I first heard Dr. Hersh present these findings.

Hersh states, "School and teacher 'effectiveness' here refers to student academic achievement tests, usually in reading and math. This is not to suggest that such schooling outcomes are the only objectives we should consider but rather that they are, for the moment, the only variables on which we can easily compare schools" (R. H. Hersh, *What Makes Some Schools and Teachers More Effective*).

Hersh goes on to say, "For the past two years I have been reviewing literature to determine what, if anything, makes some schools and teachers more effective than others. Happily, there emerges from such research a variety of clues. When put together into a coherent whole, these clues seem to make a great deal of intuitive sense. What is particularly pleasing is that different researchers in a variety of studies are reaching similar conclusions about effective schooling and that these conclusions are reinforced by school teachers and administrators who bring to research programs the critical eyes of experience.

"This conjunction of researchers' knowledge and professional educators' wisdom marks the first time in years that one might believe optimistically in the possibility of improving education in America.

SCHOOLS DO MAKE A DIFFERENCE

"During the early 1970s researchers had the public and policy makers believing that variations among schools made no difference in student learning. Although teachers' and administrators' daily lives denied such a conclusion, their protests were muted by the media and critics' ready condemnation of American schooling. Now research findings and educational reality are congruent.

"Three powerful facts have emerged. First, people run schools. How teachers, administrators, and students behave in a school setting matters and accounts heavily toward determining a school's effectiveness. Second, quality and not just quantity of effort, materials, and time is what counts. Previously researchers measured factors such as the total books in the school library, amount spent per child, and the average number of years of teacher experience. These factors have been sown to account for little difference between more and less effective schools. Third, the curriculum of the school, which includes both what is taught and how it is taught, is important.

ATTRIBUTES OF EFFECTIVE SCHOOLS

"Table 1 lists two sets of attributes associated with the most effective schools. Under the heading of 'Social Organization' are listed those items that pervade the school building. These attributes (Clear Academic and Social Behavior Goals, Order and Discipline, High Expectations, Teacher Efficacy, Pervasive Caring, Public Rewards and Incentives, Administrative Leadership, Community Support) help promote school-wide conditions for teaching and learning across all classrooms. In essence, these are necessary social conditions that help individual teachers and students to excel.

"The second heading, 'Instruction and Curriculum,' subsumes items found in the most effective classrooms. These attributes (High Academic Learning Time, Frequent and Monitored Homework, Frequent Monitoring of Student Progress, Tightly Coupled Curriculum, Variety of Teaching Strategies, Opportunities for Student Responsibility), in the context of the previously mentioned social organization factors, help promote the classroom conditions for maximum student engagement with purposeful learning activities. The line between the two sets of conditions ('Social Organization' and 'Instruction and Curriculum') is not hard and fast. In fact, they are overlapping and interactive, complementary and reciprocal to each other. Clear school-wide goals, for example, not only may help generate community understanding and support but also may allow individual teachers to better assess the fit between their expectations for students, students' expectations of themselves, and the curriculum.

SOCIAL ORGANIZATION

"Schools are social entities whose function is purposeful learning. As with all social groupings their organizational existence is dependent on adherence to some minimum common sets of values, norms, beliefs, expectations, rules, and sanctions. Rutter refers to this as a school's *ethos*. Wynne calls it *coherence*. Glass uses the word *tone*. I prefer *community*. Whatever term is selected it is important to note that there is a need in a school for such shared agreements on rules and the like because it is the existence of common understanding and assent that creates the foundation for trusting and respect for others—the glue of social and moral intercourse.

"The research suggests that schools which are most effective create a distinctive sense of community within the school building, a community derived from conditions that profoundly affect how and why educators and students treat each other, how much that precious commodity time is valued, and how well academic and social learning skills are integrated.

"Clear academic and social behavior goals. Effective schools have articulated a clear school-wide set of academic and social behavior goals. Basic skills achievement in reading, writing, and mathematics is heavily emphasized across the entire teaching staff as is student behavior that promotes

Table 19.1. Attributes of Effective Schools

Social Organization	Instruction and Curriculum
Clear Academic and Social Behavior Goals	High Academic Learning Time (ALT)
Order and Discipline	Frequent and Monitored Homework
High Expectations	Frequent Monitoring of Student Progress
Teacher Efficacy	Tightly Coupled Curriculum
Pervasive Caring	Variety of Teaching Strategies
Public Rewards and Incentives	Opportunities for Student Responsibility
Administrative Leadership	
Community Support	

an orderly classroom and school climate. There is no ambiguity. Teachers, parents, and students share the same understanding of the school's goals.

"*Order and discipline.* Administrators, teachers, and students understand and agree to basic rules of conduct. Each person may expect that such rules will be uniformly enforced, be they rules against gum chewing, running in the hallway, hitting another person, or showing disregard for school property. The attitude of each teacher is that 'I have the right to enforce the rules even if the student is not in my particular class.'

"The concern for an orderly and disciplined school climate is not meant to be oppressive. The 1960s critics of oppressive schools made their point so well that the pendulum has often swung too far the other way with the result that the quest for 'open' schools and classrooms has frequently ended in near chaos. Effective schools seem to find that happy medium between too rigid and too loose discipline. The solitude of a tomb is not required but neither is the noise of a circus tolerated. Effective schools recognize order as a social necessity, not too much order as to snuff out spontaneity and individualism but enough to get on with the business of learning. When asked, students in effective schools tell you that the rules and teachers are fair, even if they don't like the rules or penalties.

"*High expectations.* Teachers and administrators in effective schools hold higher academic and social behavior expectations for their students than do teachers and administrators in less effective schools. High expectations carry several messages. First, they symbolize the demand for excellence and tell the student 'I think you ought to and can achieve.' High expectations are stars to reach for. Second, they communicate to the student that the teacher cares by saying, in effect, 'The reason I have high expectations for you is that I care about you.' Third, high expectations serve as the adult world's professional judgment, which is translated by the student as 'I am really more capable than even I at times think I am. If my teacher continues to have high expectations for me, even when I screw up, then maybe I really can do better.'

"*Teacher efficacy.* Effective schools have a strong sense of efficacy—a belief that says, 'I know I can teach any and all of these kids.' Efficacy is a sense of potency, and it is what provides a teacher with the energy needed for relentless and persevering effort required to get many students to work. A sense of efficacy combined with high expectations for one's students communicates powerfully to students that they can learn and that they will learn, or dammit, we will both die trying!

"*Pervasive caring.* Student in effective schools tell you that their teachers and administrators care about them. One child, when asked, 'How do you know your teacher cares?' responded, 'Because she gets mad at me when I don't do my homework or do poorly on a test.'

"Caring is expressed in a variety of ways. High expectations, strict but fair enforcement of rules, and homework assignments, for example, all tell the student that the teacher is paying attention to them and cares about their achievement. Observers of effective schools see the caring atmosphere in the informal patting of children's heads, the rigorous demands of a high school English teacher symbolized by blue penciled essays, and the staff's collective celebration of student achievement. Teachers, administrators, and parents too know when a school is a caring place for students and say so when asked.

"*Public rewards and incentives.* Effective schools have a system of clear and public rewards and incentives for student achievement. Public display of excellent student work honor roll, assemblies to honor student excellence, notes sent home to parents, and verbal and nonverbal praise from teachers as often as possible serve to motivate and sustain students' achievement of a school's high expectations for them.

"*Administrative leadership.* Effective schools have administrative leaders, most often principals, who are active advocates for and facilitators of the above set of conditions. Such leadership does not mean that the principal, for example, must do the curriculum revision, or be the master teacher, or conduct the teachers' evaluation; rather, it means that the principal is a person who helps to make sure these tasks are carried out appropriately. Such a person listens to staff requests and seeks to support such requests whenever reasonable. Such a person initiates dialogues concerning expectations, school-wide rules, and the establishment of a good testing program. Most essentially, with such leadership, the administration is seen by both teachers and students as supportive, caring, and trustworthy, all of which helps create conditions for excellence.

"*Community support.* Effective schools have been found to have more parent and community contact than less effective schools. Contact with parents is not limited to concerns of truancy or misbehavior. Parents and other community members are engaged in school beautification programs, tutoring, fund-raising, and just plain being kept informed of school expectations, successes, and failures. Effective schools usually have more positive parent initiated contacts than do less effective schools.

INSTRUCTION AND CURRICULUM

"'Instruction and curriculum,' which comprises the second set of attributes in table 1 refers to the part of schooling that is most familiar to the public. For example, the results of the post-Sputnik revolution in schooling (with its increased emphasis on math and science, its extension into the new curricula, inquiry teaching, open classrooms, and mini-courses) were all highly visible and publicized alternations in the instructional and curricular patterns of the past two decades. Only recently have researchers begun to understand the mechanisms underlying the strengths and weaknesses of some of the components of these patterns. Clearly all the factors previously discussed as part of the social organization of the school overlap and complement the instructional curriculum. I have labeled these two sets of attributes separately only for the sake of convenience in this discussion.

"*High academic learning time (ALT)*. Not surprisingly researchers have found that up to a point the more time one spends on a learning task the more one learns. Although this sounds perfectly obvious and perhaps hardly worth mentioning, this rediscovery is actually more complex and very important.

"First, researchers have found that in many classrooms teachers may allocate a great deal of instructional time (for example, reading instruction) but the students are behaviorally engaged in learning how to read (reading, reciting, doing worksheets, and so forth) for only a small fraction of the allotted time. Several studies show that second and third grade teachers might allocate two hours per day for reading instruction, but upon observation of their classrooms, one could see students spending an average of only twelve to fifteen minutes a day in learning how to read! Thus, allocated time, or teachers' intended time for instruction, has been shown not to be the best indicator of what covers effective instruction.

"Consequently, a more precise measure of time has been substituted for allocated time. Called 'time on task,' this is a measure of how much time students actually are engaged in the study of a particular subject or skill. However, although this measure approximates more closely the actual time a student spends on a learning activity, it does not reveal whether or not the student is successfully learning while engaged in that learning task. Imagine a student who has great perseverance and spends many hours in class trying to read a history book that is four grade levels above his reading level. Clearly this mismatch of instructional material and time on task would not correlate with effective, much less efficient, learning.

"Finally, therefore, researchers have arrived at the notion of Academic Learning Time (ALT). This is the amount of time a student actually spends on a learning activity in which he or she is achieving a high rate of success (90 percent or better) at that task. ALT takes into account the amount of time well spent and requires assessment not only of the time dimension but also of the appropriateness of the curriculum and measures of success. The key research finding here is that effective schools have much higher ALT ratios than do less effective schools. This means that not only do teachers in more effective schools waste less class time in starting and ending instructional activities but they select curriculum materials that are most appropriate to student abilities.

"(Ten minutes of lost instruction in each high school class per day totals at least one hour of lost instruction every day, 180 hours per year, over 500 hours for three years of high school. Given that an average high school course requires about 180 to 200 hours of in-class instruction per year, 500 lost hours is considerable.)

"Frequent and monitored homework. Teachers in effective schools, after fourth grade, require more homework more often and provide students with feedback about how well their homework was completed. Homework, up to a point, tells the student that learning is more than just a school-room activity that expectations go beyond minimum effort, and that independent learning is valued. Perhaps equally important, homework increases ALT. By checking homework and providing students feedback, teachers tell students that they care about whether or not it is done (part of the incentive and caring dimension of schooling) as well as find out how well the students are learning on their own.

"Frequent monitoring of student progress. Administrators and teachers in effective schools monitor student academic progress more frequently than do staffs in less effective schools. Such monitoring consists of a combination of more frequent classroom tests and quizzes: formal and informal; written and oral; school-wide, district-wide, and national. Most emphasis is placed on frequent in-class monitoring coupled with direct and immediate feedback to students. Such frequent monitoring serves an important diagnostic function, prevents students from falling behind, and tells students that what is being taught is important.

"Tightly coupled curriculum. Effective schools have a curriculum closely related to both school-wide and individual grade-level objectives. Teachers do not rely solely on commercial products but tailor or create materials and activities to meet the agreed upon goals. The need for a tight connection between curriculum and objectives is perhaps best illustrated by a recent study. Researchers found that the five most widely used standardized test items in the U.S., in fourth-grade math, had no more than 60 percent correspondence with any of the three most popular selling fourth-grade math textbook series. Effective schools purposely link goals, curriculum, and evaluation devices in a tightly coupled way to avoid the common mismatch in testing and teaching.

"Variety of teaching strategies. Several studies have found that teachers in effective schools use a greater variety of teaching strategies than teachers in less effective schools. That is, teachers in effective schools are able to accommodate better to student differences (as measured by frequent evaluation) by employing an alternative teaching strategy when students do not seem to be succeeding.

"Opportunities for student responsibility. Effective schools provide students with more opportunities for engaging in responsible behaviors. Such

opportunities include student government, hallway monitors, discipline panels, peer and cross-age tutoring, and school fund raising projects.

CUMULATIVE EFFECTS

"Each of the attributes above has been shown separately to exist in some effective school studies. However, it is important to note that simply creating one, two, or three of such conditions at random would not necessarily result in a more effective school, measured at least in academic achievement terms. The more important conclusion that one draws from the research is that it is the cumulative effects of these conditions that has payoff. Although no one has shown which ones or how many of the above conditions are necessary and sufficient to guarantee an effective school, observers of such schools suggest that there is an element of synergy involved.

"That is, it seems that one has to do many things at once to do one thing well. It would be folly, for instance, to believe that simply increasing teacher expectations for students would necessarily lead to increase ALT or teacher efficacy. But in combination, many of the attributes above may help create a critical mass of conditions that serve to better promote student achievement. We are unsure as yet as to what variables such a critical mass comprises, but the story of Marva Collins, a Chicago elementary teacher recently portrayed on CBS's '60 Minutes,' perhaps illustrates the point to be made here.

"A Chicago elementary teacher for ten years, Ms. Collins by her own admission had failed in her attempt to teach black children in Chicago's public schools. So she quit, only to open her own thirty-five-pupil school in her house. The '60 Minutes' program shows her as the supremely successful teacher in her new setting, and it is instructive to note her new teaching conditions. First, the children were sent by parents who chose her school, and most paid extra for the privilege. Second, the students knew they could and would be expelled if their behavior did not match the teacher's standards. Third, Ms. Collins was a bear for time on task, eliminating recess and such 'frills' as physical education. Fourth, she held very high expectations. Fifth, she had a high sense of efficacy.

SUMMARY

"The best summary of this literature was recently articulated by Tommy Tomlinson in a Phi Delta Kappan article. He states that school resources are not the first or generic cause of learning.

"The ability and effort of the child is the prime cause, and the task of the schools is to enable children to use their abilities and efforts in the most efficient and effective manner. In the last analysis, that translates as undistracted work, and neither schools nor research have discovered methods or resources that obviate this fact. We should take comfort from the emerging evidence: it signifies a situation we can alter. The common thread of meaning in all that research has disclosed tells us that academically effective schools are 'merely' schools organized on behalf of the consistent and undeviating pursuit of learning. The parties to the enterprise—principals, teachers, parents and fait accompli students—coalesce on the purpose, justification and methods of schooling. Their common energies are spent on teaching and learning in a systematic fashion. They are serious about, even dedicated to, the proposition that children can and shall learn in schools. No special treatment and no magic, just the provision of the necessary conditions for learning.

"Tomlinson reminds us that in the end it is what students do that ultimately causes student achievement. All the conditions, all of the attributes I have discussed are the context for maximizing student effort.

"Finally, I find it hopeful that the conditions for effective schooling are in our control, that, more than money, it is a will for excellence that may best serve as the catalyst for school improvement" (Hersh, *What Makes Some Schools and Teachers More Effective*, pp. 1–5).

(A three-page bibliography of the research studies reviewed by Dr. Hersh is available upon request by writing to Editor, Oregon School Study Council, University of Oregon, Eugene, OR 97401.)

Chapter 20

The Common Principles of Essential Schools

1. Learning to use one's mind well
2. Less is more, depth over coverage
3. Goals apply to all students
4. Personalization
5. Student-as-worker, teacher-as-coach
6. Demonstration of mastery
7. A tone of decency and trust
8. Commitment to the entire school
9. Resources dedicated to teaching and learning
10. Democracy and equity

For 25 years, the Coalition of Essential Schools (CES) has been at the forefront of creating and sustaining personalized, equitable, and intellectually challenging schools. Guided by a set of common principles, essential schools are places of powerful student learning where all students have the chance to reach their full potential. Diverse in size, population, and programmatic emphasis, essential schools serve K–12 students in urban, suburban, and rural communities.

THE CES COMMON PRINCIPLES

The CES Common Principles, based on decades of research and practice, are a guiding philosophy rather than a replicable model for schools. This research and practice reflects the wisdom of thousands of educators who are successfully engaged in creating personalized, equitable, and academically challenging schools for all young people. The CES Common Principles describe the core beliefs and characteristics of essential schools and work in tandem with the CES Benchmarks (found at www.essentialschools.org/items/5), which describe resulting practices that successfully bolster student achievement.

Learning to Use One's Mind Well

The school should focus on helping young people learn to use their minds well. Schools should not be comprehensive if such a claim is made at the expense of the school's central intellectual purpose.

Less Is More, Depth Over Coverage

The school's goals should be simple: that each student master a limited number of essential skills and areas of knowledge. While these skills and areas will, to varying degrees, reflect the traditional academic disciplines, the program's design should be shaped by the intellectual and imaginative powers and competencies that the students need, rather than by "subjects" as conventionally defined. The aphorism "less is more" should dominate: curricular decisions should be guided by the aim of thorough student mastery and achievement rather than by an effort to merely cover content.

Goals Apply to All Students

The school's goals should apply to all students, while the means to these goals will vary as those students themselves vary. School practice should be tailor-made to meet the needs of every group or class of students.

Personalization

Teaching and learning should be personalized to the maximum feasible extent. Efforts should be directed toward a goal that no teacher have direct responsibility for more than 80 students in the high school and middle school and no more than 20 in the elementary school. To capitalize on this personalization, decisions about the details of the course of study, the use of students' and teachers' time and the choice of teaching materials and specific pedagogies must be unreservedly placed in the hands of the principal and staff.

Student-as-Worker, Teacher-as-Coach

The governing practical metaphor of the school should be student-as-worker, rather than the more familiar metaphor of teacher-as-deliverer-of-instructional-services. Accordingly, a prominent pedagogy will be coaching, to provoke students to learn how to learn and thus to teach themselves.

Demonstration of Mastery

Teaching and learning should be documented and assessed with tools based on student performance of real tasks. Students not yet at appropriate levels of competence should be provided intensive support and resources to assist them quickly to meet those standards. Multiple forms of evidence, ranging from ongoing observation of the learner to completion of specific projects, should be used to better understand the learner's strengths and needs, and to plan for further assistance. Students should have opportunities to exhibit their expertise before family and community. The diploma should be awarded upon a successful final demonstration of mastery for graduation—an exhibition. As the diploma is awarded when earned, the school's program proceeds with no strict age grading and with no system of credits earned by "time spent" in class. The emphasis is on the students' demonstration that they can do important things.

A Tone of Decency and Trust

The tone of the school should explicitly and self-consciously stress values of unanimous expectation ("I won't threaten you, but I expect much of you"), of trust (until abused), and of decency (the values of fairness, generosity, and tolerance). Incentives appropriate to the school's particular students and teachers should be emphasized. Parents should be key collaborators and vital members of the school community.

Commitment to the Entire School

The principal and teachers should perceive themselves as generalists first (teachers and scholars in general education) and specialists second (experts in but one particular discipline). Staff should expect multiple obligations (teacher-counselor-manager) and a sense of commitment to the entire school.

Resources Dedicated to Teaching and Learning

Ultimate administrative and budget targets should include student loads that promote personalization, substantial time for collective planning by teachers, competitive salaries for staff, and an ultimate per pupil cost not to exceed that at traditional schools by more than 10 percent. To accomplish this, administrative plans may have to show the phased reduction or elimination of some services now provided students in many traditional schools.

Democracy and Equity

The school should demonstrate non-discriminatory and inclusive policies, practices, and pedagogies. It should model democratic practices that involve all who are directly affected by the school. The school should honor diversity and build on the strength of its communities, deliberately and explicitly challenging all forms of inequity.

**This list of principles is taken from Coalition of Essential Schools, 2011, www.essentialschools.org/items/4.

Chapter 21

Summary

We are about to enter an exciting and dynamic new era of change in our public school system and process of education. The coming changes will be challenges and opportunities in disguise. Making the changes suggested in this book will require hard work, focused dedication to educational excellence with practical applications, and a strong commitment to reestablishing America as a world leader in education and learning.

The older, 1992 *Saving America's Children* report used as a basis for this book by written permission was developed by some of the very best American and international educators; they are practitioners, not just theorists. Along with the updated contributions of this author gained through extensive study and practical experience, this book details what is needed and must be implemented if we ever hope to have our children achieve or exceed international academic standards.

We have the resources. We must now demonstrate to ourselves and the rest of the world that we also have the positive attitude and will to change, because failure for America's children is simply not an option. We must leave a legacy our children can build on.

Join me in leaving a real legacy: saving America's kids! Over the past two years, I've been reading, thinking, praying, and writing a lot about leaving a legacy. A real legacy isn't property, buildings, or possessions. A real legacy is the influence you and I have had in people's lives. It's character demonstrated, modeled, and imitated. It's lessons learned and lived and stories told, repeated, and passed along by others we loved and touched in some way.

We're already building the legacy we will leave behind when we're gone, one decision, one action, one relationship at a time. Is what you are building what you really want to leave? This book implores you to come join me and save America's kids! Implement this blueprint for change and help achieve or exceed international standards in American schools (as adapted from Jim Stephens, *Notes from My Journey: After You Are Gone*).

I want to close by telling you a brief story about Napoleon (actually, it was Cortez, I found out later) that I related to the staff at Perrydale School in a memo as we were striving to make necessary changes to keep from having to consolidate with a neighboring district and to meet or exceed international standards together in 1996:

> I am reminded of this story about Napoleon that demonstrates the kind of attitude I believe that we need to have in Perrydale at this particular time. This story is about strategic planning, all-out commitment, teamwork, overcoming obstacles, and solving problems.
>
> When Napoleon landed for an important battle, he is reported to have turned around to his captains and said, "Captains, burn your ships!" When the captains questioned his orders and asked why, Napoleon said, "The only way you are going to win this battle is by going home in the ships of your enemies." The captains then understood the kind of passion and burning desire and commitment it was going to take to win and to overcome their enemies (their obstacles, their problems, their challenges to reach international education standards) (Adsit, 1996; Andrews, 1992).

We may have some conflict and stress! Conflict and stress are OK! We can resolve conflict and stress in an adult-like, professional manner. Communicate openly with each other, trust each other, attentively listen to each other, mutually respect each other, care about each other, remain open minded, love each other, and, in the end, do what is best for kids!

I implore all of you reading this book, and all of America's public schools, save America's kids and do what is best for our kids by implementing this strategic plan for reaching or exceeding international educational standards. The plan works! The question is, will you work the plan?

References

Adsit, Tim L. (February 28, 1996). Excerpt from memo to all certified, classified, administrative, and confidential staff. "Captains Burn Your Ships—A Story about Napoleon." Perrydale School District No. 21, Perrydale (Amity), Oregon. (Story from Andy Andrews (1992), *Burn the Boats*, Nashville: First Image.)
———. (2011). *Small Schools, Education, and the Importance of Community: Pathways for Improvement and a Sustainable Future.* Lanham, MD: Rowman & Littlefield Education in partnership with Association of School Business Officials International.
Adsit, Tim L., and Murdock, George. (2005). *Practical Ideas for Cutting Costs and Ways to Generate Alternative Revenue Sources.* Lanham, MD: Rowman & Littlefield Education in partnership with Association of School Business Officials International.
———. (2011). *Cutting Costs and Generating Revenues in Education.* Lanham, MD: Rowman & Littlefield, in partnership with the Association of School Business Officials International.
Bender, Texas Bix. (1992). *Don't Squat With Yer Spurs On: A Cowboy's Guide to Life.* Layton, UT: Gibbs-Smith Publisher.
Berliner, D. (September 1983). "The Executive Functions of Teaching." *The Instructor*, Vol. 93, No. 2, pp. 28–40.
Blum, Richard E. (1984). *Effective Schooling Practices: A Research Synthesis—Onward to Excellence: Making Schools More Effective.* Portland, OR: Education Northwest (formerly Northwest Regional Educational Laboratory). http://educationnorthwest.org/contact.
Brophy, J. (1979). "Teacher Behavior and Its Effects." *Journal of Educational Psychology*, Vol. 71, No. 6, pp. 733–50.
Brown, D. S. (1988). "Twelve Middle-School Teachers Planning." *Elementary School Journal*, Vol. 89, No. 1, pp. 69–87.
Coalition of Essential Schools. (2011). http://www.essentialschools.org/items/4.

"Competing in the New International Economy." Washington, DC: Office of Technology Assessment, 1990. http://www.uni.edu/darrow/frames/scans.html.

Condon, D., and Maggs, A. (1986). "Direct Instruction Research: An International Focus." *International Journal of Special Education*, Vol. 1, pp. 35–47.

Daggett, Willard. (1992). *Saving America's Children: Achieving International Standards in American Schools—A Blueprint for Change.* Presented by Associated Oregon Industries and The National Association for Schools of Excellence, 1992, p. 2.

Doyle, W. (1984). "Effective Classroom Practices for Secondary Schools." *R & D Report* No. 619:1. Austin: Texas University Research and Development Center for Teacher Education.

Education Up Close. (August 2006). "What Works in the Classroom: The McREL Report in a Nutshell." www.glencoe.com/sec/teachingtoday/educationupclose.phtml/6.

Gagne, E. D. (1985). "Strategies for Effective Teaching and Learning." In *The Cognitive Psychology of School Learning.* Boston: Little, Brown.

Gagne, R. M., and Briggs, L. J. (1974). *Principles of Instructional Design.* New York: Holt, Rinehart & Winston.

Garrabrandt, Bruce. (2004). *The Power of Having Desire: The Secret to Accomplishing Anything You Really Want.* Hummelstown, PA: Possibility Press.

Gerston, R. (1986). "Direct Instruction: A Research-Based Approach to Curriculum Design and Teaching." *Exceptional Children*, Vol. 53, No. 1, pp. 17–31.

Giblin, Les. (1956). *How to Have Confidence and Power in Dealing with People.* Englewood Cliffs, NJ: Prentice-Hall, Inc.

Hawley, W., and Rosenholtz, S., with Goodstein, H., and Hasselbring, T. (Summer 1984). "Good Schools: What Research Says About Improving Student Achievement." *Peabody Journal of Education*, Vol. 61, No. 4.

Hersh, Robert H. (Winter 1982). *What Makes Some Schools and Teachers More Effective?* Oregon School Study Council, University of Oregon, Eugene.

Hord, S., Rutherford, W., Huling-Austin, L., and Hall, G. (1998). *Taking Charge of Change.* Austin, TX: Southwest Educational Development Laboratory.

Hostrop, Richard W. (1975). *Managing Education for Results.* Palm Springs, CA: ETC Publications.

Hunter, Madeline. (1994). "Planning for Effective Instruction: Lesson Design." In *Enhancing Teaching* (pp. 87–95). New York: Macmillan

Kallison, J. M. (1986). "Effects of Lesson Organization on Achievement." *American Educational Research Journal*, Vol. 23, No. 2, pp. 337–47.

Koretz, D. (2009). "How Do American Students Measure Up? Making Sense of International Comparisons." WikiBooks, December 27, 2010. http//en.wikibooks.org/wiki/InvestigatingCritical_526_Contemporary_Issues_in_Education/Student_Academic_Performance.

Kriegel, R. J., and Patler, L. (1991). *If It Ain't Broke, Break It!* New York: Warner Books.

The Learning Pyramid. Adapted from National Training Laboratories, Bethel, Maine.

Marzano, R. J., Gaddy, B. B., and Dean, C. (2000). *What Works in Classroom Instruction.* Aurora, CO: Mid-continent Research for Education and Learning.

Moore, J. (1986). "Direct Instruction: A Model of Instructional Design." *Educational Psychology*, Vol. 6, 201–29.

Pascarelli, J.T. (February 1985). *Conditions of Readiness to Change.* Portland, OR: Northwest Regional Educational Laboratory.

Phillips, Donald T. (1992). *Lincoln on Leadership: Executive Strategies for Tough Times.* New York: Warner Books.

———. (1997). *The Founding Fathers on Leadership: Classic Teamwork in Changing Times.* New York: Warner Books.

Pratton, J., and Hates, L. W. (1985). "The Effects of Active Participation on Student Learning." *Journal of Educational Research*, Vol. 79, 210–15.

Quality Education Commission Report 2010. www.ode.state.or.us.

Rosenshine, B., and Stevens, R. (1986). "Teaching Functions." In M. C. Wittrock (Ed.), *Handbook of Research on Training* (3rd ed., pp. 375–91). New York: Macmillan.

Rosetta Stone. www.bn.com/rosettastone.

Saving America's Children: Achieving International Standards in American Schools—A Blueprint for Change. (1992). Portland, OR: Associated Oregon Industries and National Association for Schools of Excellence.

Schuller, Robert H., Sr. (1983). *Tough Times Never Last, But Tough People Do!* Nashville, TN: Thomas Nelson.

Schwartz, David J. (1959, 1965). *The Magic of Thinking Big.* New York: Simon & Schuster.

Schwarzkopf, H. Norman. (1992). *The Autobiography: It Doesn't Take A Hero.* New York: Bantam Books.

Scoresby, A. Lynn. (2001). *Character and Competence: Developing Character and Improving Achievement.* Orem, UT: Knowledge Gain Publications.

Skills and Tasks for Jobs: A SCANS Report for America 2000. (1999). Washington, DC: The Secretary's Commission on Achieving Necessary Skills, U.S. Department of Labor.

Stallings, J. (1980). "Allocated Academic Learning Time Revisited, or Beyond Time on Task." *Educational Researcher*, Vol. 9, No. 11, pp. 11–16.

Stephens, Jim. (2011). *Notes from My Journey: After You Are Gone.* http://www.jimstephens.com/2011/03/16/after-you-are-gone/.

Walberg, H. J. (1984). "What Makes Schooling Effective? A Synthesis and a Critique of Three National Studies." *Contemporary Education: A Journal of Reviews*, Vol. 1, No. 1, pp. 23–34.

What Work Requires of Schools: A SCANS Report for America 2000. (June 1991). Washington, DC: The Secretary's Commission on Achieving Necessary Skills, U.S. Department of Labor.

What Works: Research about Teaching and Learning, second edition. (1987). Washington, DC: U.S. Department of Education.

About the Author

Tim L. Adsit has excelled as a "change agent" throughout his career to date and served as a professional executive administrator in school districts that value visionary leadership and continuous improvement in student learning and achievement.

Tim is uniquely qualified to write this book by a record of successful and progressively responsible service in the positions of superintendent; director of curriculum, instruction, school improvement, assessment, personnel services, rural schools, interim special education, and grant writing; management consultant; elementary and secondary principal; high school, middle school, and elementary school teacher; private Christian school executive administrator and principal; college graduate teaching assistant; and adjunct summer visiting professor. These roles illustrate the ability to play a dynamic leadership role in the field of education. He possesses a broad knowledge of all phases of educational administration and brings diverse, demonstrated, successful experience ranging from public and private school districts as small as 60 students to as large as 12,500 students. He also has had experience serving as superintendent and principal in one of the largest public boarding schools in the nation.

More recently, he has started two small businesses of his own, which you can get more detailed information about at www.tlawinc.vpweb.com and www.nexusinc.vpweb.com if you are interested.

Tim received his M.Ed. and B.S. in education from Oregon State University and did post-graduate work in educational administration at the University of Oregon. He also received his Doctor of Divinity in December of 2009 from Cambridge Theological Seminary. Tim and his wife, Maggie, reside in Bend, Oregon. Should you wish to contact the author, you may reach him at timads@bendbroadband.com or call his office at 1-541-383-5119.

www.ingramcontent.com/pod-product-compliance
Lightning Source LLC
Chambersburg PA
CBHW060536250426
43668CB00051B/1774